Pige

Animal
Series editor: Jonathan Burt

Pigeon

Barbara Allen

REAKTION BOOKS

*For David, for Rhys (thank you for bringing home an injured squab during
the writing of this book), and for my feathered friends, named (Bacardi,
Chagall, Bert, Celeste, O*[...] *and Splash) and unnamed; you are
truly magnificent!*

Published by

REAKTION BOOKS LTD
33 Great Sutton Street
London EC1V ODX, UK
www.reaktionbooks.co.u[...]

First published 2009
Copyright © Barbara All[...]

This book has been published with the assistance of the Australian
Academy of the Humanities

Printed and bound in China by C&C Offset Printing Co., Ltd

British Library Cataloguing in Publication Data
Allen, Barbara
    Pigeon. – (Animal)
    1. Pigeons 2. Pigeons – Social aspects. 3. Pigeons in literature.
    I. Title II. Series
    598.6'5-DC22

ISBN: 978 1 86189 513 4

Contents

Introduction

In the Foreword to Carl Naether's *The Book of the Pigeon and of Wild Foreign Doves*, Naether writes: 'Long before I began actual work on the manuscript, a prominent fancier forewarned me: "Don't you know that no pigeon book has ever become a best seller?"'[1] He continues, quoting other advice he had received: "'Most of your effort and time will be thrown away. I have never yet seen a pigeon book that paid for its printing and effort . . . I have seen many start pigeon books but precious few finish them."'[2]

Most days I walk past the couple, on my way to the shopping centre. On a small side street, where little cottages undergo renovation, and warehouses are being converted into expensive places of residence . . . they are there, resting, under a tree. Two pigeons, unremarkable perhaps, yet part of the landscape; a lesson in loyalty and resilience. The female has a problem with one leg, so she is more often than not sitting, while the male struts around her, cooing softly. They are well fed; the local workmen leave the remains of their lunch for them and in one of the cottages I have seen an elderly man come out and feed them crusts in the evening. Every now and again, a plastic, disused takeaway container is filled with water for them. All this, on the edge of affluence; the ordinary.

Pigeons; as I am writing this I can hear cooing in my garden. In the mornings I feed two rock pigeons, and the gatecrashers: the collared doves.

Ayuda a los refugiados, contribuye a la paz.

Alto Comisionado de las Naciones Unidas para los Refugiados

United Nations General Assembly

Second Special Session On Disarmament   May 1982

CENTRO REGIONAL DE LAS NACIONES UNIDAS
PARA LA PAZ, EL DESARME Y EL DESARROLLO
EN AMERICA LATINA Y EL CARIBE   Lima, Perú

Pigeons fascinate me. They have been our co-workers, delivering messages, helping during wartime, a source of food, a sport and obsession for many, and a suitable religious sacrifice. They have been winged messengers through the ages, relaying results from the early Olympic Games, football games and examinations. They have helped us unravel some of the mysteries of genetics and of navigation. Pigeons are similar to many in society: on the edge, unnoticed, yet vital in the history of civilization. But they are a paradox; doves are from the same family as the pigeon, yet they elicit quite different reactions. 'Stool pigeon' and 'pigeon-toed' are phrases with negative connotations, whereas if we 'dovetail' something, that gauges a more positive response. These 'rats with wings' became the symbol of peace. Would the United Nations change its 'dove' to a 'pigeon'? Would the manufacturers of Dove soap increase its sales by renaming their products Pigeon? What about Dove chocolate? Would we accord the same respect to the Bank of America and to Visa credit cards, both of which have doves as part of their logo, if we said they were pigeons? What about Christmas cards adorned with grey rock pigeons instead of white 'doves', or feral pigeons being released at a wedding, instead of pigeons that lack pigment? Having said that, some companies are using the word pigeon. There is a new line of baby/mothercare products from Asia called Pigeon, and a successful clothing label, Pigeon Combine (the clothing tends to be of two shades, grey and black, hence the name).

The difference between the emotional reactions caused by these two birds is quite remarkable. In Japan, a thousand doves are released as part of the anniversary ceremonies marking Hiroshima Day. In Britain, the city of London is bent on culling the pigeons from Trafalgar Square. These two birds from the same family are viewed quite differently.[3]

The relationship that humans have with the pigeon is one of the oldest partnerships. The bond between human and bird, feather, skin, wing and finger, is exquisite in its intensity and in its earthiness. There are no diamanté collars or luxury bedding for the humble pigeon. Pet food companies have been unable to cash in by promoting 'pigeon treats' or 'gourmet delights'. One could argue that these are unnecessary, superfluous; these birds are motivated by the basic or core ingredients for living, as well as dependent on their unique capabilities, as evidenced by the homing skills of the racing pigeon. They may come without the glitter and commercial value (though some make big bucks for their racing owners), but this does not mean that they are without their devotees and their admirers. Ask pigeon fanciers why they breed or race them and see the delight in their eyes as they try to define the reasons in a few words. It is not solely for fame and a little wealth; there is something special about the relationship between the owner and his or her bird. This fascination unites people from diverse backgrounds and experiences, including Roy Rogers, Mike Tyson and Yul Brynner. The eponymous hero of the popular British cartoon strip *Andy Capp* was a working class character who was, among other things, a pigeon fancier.

Robert Wright Campbell suggests that the basis of this admiration may have its origin in an acknowledgement of (or at least a recognition of) commonality; pigeons and humans have much in common, and, disturbingly, pigeons hold fast to certain qualities that we humans tend to let slide:

> People and pigeons are curiously much alike. That is to say the lovely birds have those qualities of fidelity, affection, and love, courage, determination, and pride which are qualities humans may boast of when they are at their

Pigeons on the Pilsudski Monument, Lublin.

best. If they display jealousy and pettishness, quarrelsome moments and gluttony they should be forgiven, for their sins are small . . . In some things they shame us, by and large. Once mated, they are wed for life unless forcibly separated. When set to the task, such as a long race, they will persevere and endure through measures of hell that only the best of men will willingly undertake.[4]

I suggest there are other, more allusive facets to this fascination: denial and dreams. The pigeon symbolizes who we are, whereas the dove represents the 'other', who we would like to be. As the pigeon and the dove belong to the same family, so too do these two birds represent aspects of the one, or same, personality. The pigeon is the 'ordinary', the 'everyperson', who we are in our daily lives. The dove, on the other hand, speaks to our hearts, opens the envelope of our dreams. The dove is what we aspire to, what we fantasize about becoming; she is our deepest desires coming into being. She is magnificent, beautiful, exquisite: often out of reach, never to be realized.

We see this dichotomy played out in literature and media; the musical *My Fair Lady* is a classic pigeon to dove story. Eliza Doolittle is transformed from the ordinary (the pigeon: despised, frowned upon, unnoticed) to the breathtaking (the dove: admired, courted, extraordinary).

Pigeons live in a range of different habitats, including cities, coastal cliffs and bushland.

Colombe bleu Verdin.

COLUMBA CYANOVIRENS *Less, gar.*

Imp. de Coban

There are, of course, examples where this is overturned. In the film *Mary Poppins*, the bird lady strikes a chord and moves us to tears when she sings 'Feed the birds, tuppence a bag'. We are invited to reach deep into our souls to remember our innocence. The song with its pathos, reminds us that we are to care for the little ones, the overlooked, the 'birds' on our streets. In *Sesame Street*, Bert, the serious or 'straight' puppet, brings the love of pigeons to a new dimension, and, as a consequence, to a receptive audience. He dances with a pigeon, with choreographed moves to imitate the strut, while singing 'Doin' the pigeon'. Bert plays draughts with a pigeon (and loses because the pigeon is smarter than he is). Perhaps the pigeon was included in *Sesame Street* because pigeons are often the first animal, or 'other', that a child notices. Sometimes local pigeons are adopted as 'their' pet. *Sesame Street* is set in a city of high-rise buildings. Pigeons are plentiful in these surroundings, as the tall buildings are the closest they have to the cliffs and high places they were used to in their past. They are cliff dwellers, and what better place to live than a towering metropolis? Acknowledgement of the importance of the 'other' in children's lives is paramount in fostering respect for others (including all creation). Perhaps the use of the pigeon was a conscious ploy to represent the 'voiceless' or the 'overlooked', which is often the plight of the child.

Who can doubt the beauty of the pigeon? Proust talks of 'scattering the pigeons, whose beautiful, iridescent bodies (shaped like hearts and, as it were, the lilacs of the feathered kingdom) took refuge.'[5] Arrow-pointed, Beak Wattle, Bishaped, Handkerchief Marking, Jewing, Laced, Muffed, Oyster-eye, Shell Crown, Slippered, Stockings, Tippet (ruff or hood of the Jacobin), Tysy, Veil: these are some of the poetic terms used by pigeon breeders. How can these words sit alongside 'rats with wings'?

'Colombe bleu verdin', *Columba cyanovirens*. Engraving by César Macret after Madame Knip, from her *Les Pigeons* (Paris, 1811).

Perhaps the dilemma rests not with the pigeon/dove but ultimately with ourselves. Maybe the pigeon is really the magician's hat: we pretend that we do not see the common, ordinary hat. Instead, our hearts imagine what we want to see: a top hat complete with snow-white doves flying upwards, our dreams soaring with them.

1 Pigeon or Dove?

Is there interest in the ordinary pigeon?[1] Charles Darwin, himself a pigeon fancier, wrote about the pigeon in *Origin of Species*. When Darwin's publisher submitted the manuscript of the book to a referee for an opinion, the referee wrote back regretting that Darwin had not simply written a book on pigeon-breeding: 'Everybody is interested in pigeons', he insisted. 'The book would be reviewed in every journal in the kingdom, and would soon be on every library table.'[2]

What is it that attracts one to pigeons or doves, or any bird, for that matter? Is it the variety of types, from the small collared dove to the exotic Victoria Crowned Pigeon, from the Old Dutch Capuchine to the Franconian Trumpeter? Is it a fascination with homing instincts and the adrenalin rush associated with sporting activities? Is it because of the beauty of flight and our own yearning to soar, or is the answer to be found closer to home, that birds represent the 'other'?

It is not their ability to fly that distinguishes birds from all other animals (for insects and bats fly, and there are several species of birds that cannot fly), but the startling fact that only birds have feathers. The two most highly developed vertebrate groups, birds and mammals, both evolved independently from reptiles. The earliest fossil of a bird, estimated to be 140 million years old, is the Archaeopteryx ('ancient wing'). Its long, tapering

tail, claws and teeth are all characteristics of a reptile. What distinguished it from reptiles, though, were its wings with well-developed feathers. The Archaeopteryx was about the size of a crow, and it may have evolved from a small running dinosaur. It was probably a poor flyer. Over the past 140 million years, many bird groups have emerged, the success of their evolution due to three factors: homoiothermy, flight and successful breeding.

Feathers, which function to provide both strength and flexibility, are a reminder of its origin. Feathers probably evolved from the scales of reptiles, for they are formed from the same hard material, keratin. The skin of the pigeon harks back to its reptilian days, for reptile-like scales are found on its legs and feet, and its claws and horny beak are like modified scales.

How old is the pigeon? When trying to determine age, fossils are usually a good guide. Columbids, however, are not well represented in fossils. No truly primitive forms have been found to date. The genus *Gerandia*, which most likely belongs to the *Columbinae*, has been found in Early Miocene deposits in France, and in New Zealand fragmentary remains of a pigeon have been found from the Early/Middle Miocene. In North America, some fossil remains from the Pliocene epoch have been unearthed, and fossil remains from the Ice Age have been discovered in several regions of the world.

Reconstruction of the Archaeopteryx.

When we examine the biological facts, starting at what should be the least controversial, defining the differences between 'dove' and 'pigeon', we are confronted by the disturbing news that there is no zoological distinction between them. 'Pigeon' is the term that is usually applied to the larger species, and 'dove' to the smaller ones, but they are of the same family, the family Columbidae. This may come as a surprise, for many regard pigeons as pests yet see doves as symbols of higher virtues, such as peace and love. In the Museum of Tolerance in Los Angeles, there are two doors that block entry to the exhibition. One door is marked 'prejudice'; the other 'unprejudice'. When one tries to open the door 'unprejudice', a light comes on and a recording: 'Think . . . now use the other door.' We all harbour prejudice. Prejudice can be levelled at firmly held views concerning the humble pigeon. Substitute 'dove' and note if opinions change.

Some blame for the confusion can be placed at the feet of etymology, as well as the history of the battlefield. *Columba livia*, the scientific name for the pigeon, translates as 'the dove or diver bird of leaden or blue-grey colour'.[3] The term 'diver bird' was in part a reference to the manner in which the male bird bobs or 'bows' his head during the courtship ritual. The use of the name 'diver bird' is ancient; it is the earliest meaning of *Kolumbis* in Greek, *Columba* in Latin and *dove* in Anglo-Saxon.[4] From *Columba* comes another name for a dovecote: the 'columbarium'. The word is used in early documents, and has variants in different geographical localities: 'colomendy' in Wales and 'clummier' in Cornwall.[5] Later, we note the Anglo-Saxon variant, *culver, culvar* or *culfre*. This term survived and is evident in the place names of south-western England, giving rise to Culverhill, Culverfield and Culverwell.[6] 'Pigeon' may come from *pipio*, Latin for a young, chirping bird.[7] Some writers

A Nilgiri wood pigeon, painted on mica.

have proposed that the interchangeability of the terms 'pigeon' and 'dove' results from the Norman Conquest of Anglo-Saxon England, with French being the language of the court and of the table. 'Pigeon' was a French word, imitating the piping cries of the squabs that were kept nearby in the barn as a food source. The bigger doves were usually the ones used in 'pigeon' pie; hence the new French name 'pigeon' was used, rather

'The Turtle of Carolina', from Mark Catesby, *The Natural History of Carolina, Florida and the Bahama Islands*...vol. I (London, 1731).

than 'dove'.[8] *Dove*, on the other hand, has Saxon roots, as well as being of Norse origin. It first appeared during the time of Chaucer as *duva* or *douve*. Its young, *squab*, comes from the Norse *skvabb*, meaning 'soft and thick'.[9] *Dove* became *duffus* in East Anglia, *ducket* in the north of England and *doocot* in Scotland. *Dove* still had connections with the kitchen; in other languages similar words mean 'deaf' or 'blind', even 'dumb' or 'confused', which could allude to the way and ease with which these birds were captured for the table.

Other cultures used the sound the dove made for its name (similar to the use of the Latin *pipio*). For the Romans, *tur-tur* was used, for the Anglo-Saxons it became *turla* or *turtil*. In Hebrew, 'dove' is *yona*, which comes from *ānâ*, Hebrew for 'moan' or 'mourn' (perhaps alluding to the sound the birds make). The Hebrews also referred to the sound of the dove as *tor*. None of this presented a problem until the word was translated. When the first English Bible translators came across this word, they translated it as 'turtle'. This was prior to the naming of the hard-shelled amphibians.[10] To solve the problem, doves were to be known as turtledoves (the translators of the King James version erred; in Song of Songs 2:12, we read 'the voice of the turtle.')

All pigeons and doves are direct descendants of the blue rock pigeon. Charles Darwin, whose interest in pigeons sparked his theory of heredity, stood by his theory of the inheritance of acquired characteristics. Darwin wrote: 'Great as are the differences between the breeds of the pigeon, I am fully convinced that all are descended from the rock-pigeon [rock dove] *Columba livia*.'[11] In 2004 British and American ornithologists officially renamed the Rock Dove the Rock Pigeon.

There are 316 species of pigeons and doves, divided into 42 genera.[12] There are five subfamilies: Columbidae, Otidiphabinae (pheasant pigeon: 1 species), Treroninae (green and fruit doves:

124 species), Gourinae (crowned pigeons: 3 species) and Didunculinue (tooth-billed pigeon: 1 species). Close relatives of the pigeon include the sandgrouse (Pteroclidae) and waders (Charadriiformes). Pigeons and doves are found in every continent except Antarctica, with a preference for the tropics. Pigeons have a remarkable ability to adapt to a variety of different environments, being present in grasslands, deserts, forests and in many cities and towns. They have survived despite the fact that they have a number of predators, and have no means of defence apart from escape via flight.

'Turtur Auritis' Ray, from John Gould, *The Birds of Great Britain*, vol. IV (London, 1873)

Members of the Columbidae have, for the most part, stocky, compact bodies with short necks and legs (though some fancy breeds defy this). Their wings vary in shape and length. There is little difference in hue between the sexes. The bill is slender and fairly soft, the nostrils are covered with an operculum and the eyes are often brightly coloured. They don't live in trees, but prefer to nest on ledges (hence their unpopularity in Western cities), perhaps an ancient reminder of their origins, when they would live on rocky cliff ledges.

Pigeons have extraordinary flying capabilities. Powerful wings deliver lift and thrust at the same time. When pigeons fly, they raise their wings as high as possible, and then flap down, pushing down an enormous volume of air, in order to rise. When the wings are raised, the primary feathers spread apart, and these feathers individually twist to generate more lift. This power allows the pigeon to go from 0–50 kilometres per hour in seconds, and to fly non-stop for hundreds of kilometres.[13] Some pigeons can fly up to 80 kilometres per hour. This type of endurance is beyond human capabilities. Their avian respiratory system delivers oxygen directly to special air sacs deep in their bodies; these, combined with one-way lungs that prevent oxygen from mixing with carbon dioxide, enable them to absorb more oxygen than humans do.

Pigeons have finely attuned eyes and ears, which serve as guidance and warning systems. Pigeons' eyes, which register the shape and distance of close-up objects, see much more than we do. Each eye allows them to see almost behind their heads, which gives them a 340° field of vision. This allows the pigeon to search for food at their feet while at the same time keeping watch for predators far off. Occasionally people mock their head bobbing. Head bobbing, part of their courtship ritual, also aids their vision. Pigeons bob their heads for depth of perception. Their vision is

'Colombe Marine',
Columba litoralis.
Engraving by
César Macret after
Madame Knip,
from her
Les Pigeons
(Paris, 1811).

Colombe Marine

COLUMBA LITORALIS. *Mihi*

better with stationary objects; once they step forward, they need to jerk their head forward as well in order to orientate themselves.

Their eyes can detect ultraviolet radiation from the sun, even on cloudy days. This is essential for their navigation; without it, they will not fly (they do not fly at night, though some were trained to do so during World War II). Trained pigeons are being considered for use by the United States Coast Guard (USCG) after a team of researchers found that, as well as having the ability to see ultraviolet light, trained pigeons were twice as reliable as humans and much quicker at spotting red or yellow jackets in the water (92–3 per cent accuracy, compared with 30–40 per cent from human searchers[14]). Project Sea Hunt has been proposed for use at a number of Coast Guard air stations when sufficient pigeons have been trained. Project Sea Hunt has been put on hold due to federal budget cuts. In recent times the USGC's priority has been to spot 'hawks' – drug traffickers and terrorists – rather than to draw on the pigeons' unique abilities to assist in the rescue of humans lost at sea.

Pigeons also have a sensitivity to polarized light: that is, they 'see' an aspect of light that is invisible to us.[15] Pigeons' ears are highly sensitive as well; they are able to hear sounds of frequencies 200 times lower than the human range. This allows them to hear distant noises, and be aware of approaching storms and other dangers.

The pigeon has several unique attributes, one being that it is non-gallinaceous (lacking a gall bladder). Shakespeare knew of this, for Hamlet cries out: 'But am I pigeon-livered, and lack gall to make oppression bitter?'[16] Their mode of ingesting liquid is peculiar to them.[17] Pigeons drink by sucking up water into their beaks like a straw, as opposed to other birds that take sips of water and bend back their heads so that the water trickles down their throats. Gilbert White, the naturalist, observed this early on: 'Most birds drink sipping at intervals; but pigeons take a long continued draught, like quadrupeds.'[18] Another way in which pigeons differ from other birds is in the way they roost. When a pigeon roosts at night, it usually rests on one leg at a

Pigeons are possibly unique among birds in the way they take in fluids.

time. When they roost or doze, they do not turn or tuck their head 'under their wing', as do passerines and gamebirds; instead, they draw their head close to their body.

Pigeons are primarily seed-eaters. When the young pigeon starts to eat, it will pick up its first seed, drop it, then pick it up again. This is repeated several times before the seed is finally swallowed. Adult pigeons will behave in a similar manner when confronted with new foods. This behaviour continues even after a pigeon seems to have had enough to eat. Some have hypothesized that this behaviour is also a way for pigeons to correlate the type of food with its appearance.[19]

Pigeons are peaceful birds, but they will defend their territory if provoked. Serious fights are usually over nesting territory. If the pigeons are roosting, they will peck towards or coo defiantly at the other pigeons and birds, except for their mate, young or siblings. If one sees a predator, it usually does three things; it sends out a distress call, then 'freezes' before taking flight. If being chased, the pigeon will fly at great speed, trying to avoid being caught by skilful dodging and swerving movements. Pigeons will avoid locations where they have been frightened. They also display fear responses if they see a pile of pigeon feathers. This behaviour may also occur when they observe new items; perhaps a bucket on the ground, or even the way seed has been placed in a pile. Pigeons do not welcome sudden change, especially changes within their own territory.

The pigeon is a social bird; it actively seeks out the company of other pigeons, and not only for reproduction. The courtship ritual for pigeons is orderly and complex. Head nodding and the spreading of the tail are courtship behaviours common to all pigeon and dove species. This display is used by the male to attract a mate. During the nodding, the birds will look directly into the face of the other. If the hen is interested, she begins nodding her head in the cock's direction. The male begins to peck behind his wings, conveying interest in her. If she remains interested, she will reach her head out and move closer to the male, usually accompanied by a mating call. She fans her tail, whilst the male offers his beak. Then they indulge in what is known as the 'pigeon kiss': they rub their beaks together, then the hen will feed the male from her beak, or goes through the motions of doing so. Billing and cooing are crucial components of the mating ritual: 'Gilbert White,' said Merlin, 'remarks . . .

that "the language of birds is very ancient, and, like other ancient modes of speech, little is said, but much is intended."'[20]

Pigeons mate for life, and share parental duties. When pigeons have paired, and are ready to nest, they both go to choose the nest site, the male taking the lead and being the first to investigate the site and location. When both agree on the nest site, both hen and cock are involved in the collection of the nesting materials. The nest building intensifies when the female remains in the nest, allowing the male to fetch the materials. The nests are often loosely constructed and flimsy, and most do not last past one breeding season. One legend tells how the magpie, a builder of a secure nest, thought that the dove needed some help in the art of nest building. The dove, however, became bored, and protested, 'That'll doo-doo! That'll doo-ee!' (hence the coo-ing sound associated with the dove). The magpie gave up, frustrated by the dove's rather haphazard approach.[21]

After pairing and mating, the first eggs will be laid within ten days. The first egg is usually laid in the evening between 5 and 7 pm. In female pigeons, the reproductive organs are limited to the left side. The right ovary and the oviduct degenerate soon after formation. Because the hen has only one developed ovary, she can produce only one egg at a time. Approximately two days later, the second egg develops in the ovary after the first is laid. When mating has occurred, the hen stores sperm in order to fertilize this second egg. This egg is laid about 43–4 hours later, usually in the afternoon between 2 and 3 pm.[22] Laying two eggs allows the chances of survival of at least one to be high. Not having many mouths to feed increases survival rates as well. After the second egg has been laid, serious brooding begins. Brooding is shared, with the cock taking over sitting around midday. The hen usually returns to the nest mid-afternoon.

Baby pigeon.

The author Edward Lear began his career as a keen and proficient painter, working for John Gould. In one of his letters, written near the end of his life, Lear, in the manner of his nonsense verse, mentions the pigeons' habit of sharing the brooding schedule:

> Their punctuality as to their sitting on their eggs and *vice versa* I never knew of before. The males and females take their turns EXACTLY *every two hours*. Giuseppe . . . believes they have little watches under their wings, and that they wind them up at sunset, 8 P.M. standing on one foot and holding the watch in the other.[23]

Depending on the weather and on the breed, the squabs hatch from the eggs in 17 to 18 days. The hatching process takes between 15 and 30 hours. When the squabs have hatched and dried, they are fed within the first hour. Pigeons, unlike most other birds, are altricial; they require parental care for several days after hatching. The squab's beak is taken into that of the parent, who regurgitates pigeon milk and feeds it to its young for the first few days. Later, when the young are stronger, they will push into the throats of the parents, and aspirate the secretions. The young stay in the nest for up to two months, which is why we don't tend to see baby pigeons. Shakespeare made reference to the dove's reputation as a good parent, for they do not abandon the nest:

> As patient as the female dove,
> when that her golden couplets are disclosed.[24]

After two weeks, the cock takes over from the hen, as the hen is usually preoccupied with preparing for a new round of egg-laying.

> Pigeons, being city dwellers by choice, have caught the excitement of New York, and, like an executive who enjoys having two phones on his desk, a pair of pigeons like to keep two nests going at the same time. They deliberately place themselves under this sort of pressure. The pair at 813 Fifth Avenue, as I write, have two nests, both at that address. Squabs are being fed in one, eggs are being incubated in the other.[25]

Although pigeons only lay two eggs at a time, a single pair can produce fifty pigeons in twelve months.

One of the most fascinating features unique to pigeons is having a glandular crop that secretes nutritious 'pigeon milk' or 'crop milk' that is used to feed their young. While brooding, both parents develop pigeon milk. Milk production occurs in both sexes at the same time, probably as a result of the pituitary hormone, prolactin. Both feed their young on this substance for between 35 and 37 days. The substance is thick, like porridge. It is not produced in the breast but within the walls, because it is actually a degeneration of the epithelial cell structure. The lining of the crop thickens with water and nutrients, and peels off in clumps. Pigeon milk is high in fat and it contains no sugar. It has more protein and fat than is found in either cow or human milk and it contains immunities against disease. During the feeding, the parent tries to make the squab take as much of the milk as possible. Any milk that remains within the parent's throat is swallowed, regurgitated and offered again at the next feed. Pigeon milk fuels what is one of the most explosive growth rates of almost any creature on earth. It is so nutritious that squabs can double their size in 48 hours. Squabs take in almost their own body weight in pigeon milk every day. In two weeks they are half the size of their parents. In 25 days they are nearly fully grown and able to feed themselves:

Celia: Here comes Monsieur Le Beau.
Rosalind: With his mouth full of news.
Celia: Which he will put on us, as pigeons feed their young.
Rosalind: Then shall we be news-crammed.[26]

From about the sixth day, the milk is mixed with seed, as a way of weaning the chicks to solid food.

In popular culture, crop milk is mentioned in the Nintendo DS video game system, *Animal Crossing: Wild World*. One of the characters is Brewster, a pigeon, who runs 'The Roost', a café in the basement of the museum. Eventually he will ask if you want pigeon milk in your coffee. In the television series *Flavor of Love*, in the episode 'Mama York', Deelishis's dad asks for pigeon milk at a restaurant.

Fig. 31.—English Fantail.

Pigeons have feathers of different colours and groupings. The humble pigeon's colourings involve an exploration of colour inheritance. Darwin's studies of genetics and his theory of dominant and recessive genes came about, in part, by his observation of pigeons. In 1868 Darwin published a two-volume treatise in which he developed a theory of heredity which he termed 'pangenesis', outlining how use and disuse inheritance could occur. His research was based on his experiments with domesticated species.[27] Although Darwin later dropped the notion of pangenesis, he still accepted the inheritance of acquired characteristics. Darwin kept every breed of pigeon he could obtain, and was sent skins of other breeds from different regions of the world. He befriended pigeon fanciers, and belonged to two of London's pigeon clubs. He particularly enjoyed visiting a gin palace near Borough Market where a pigeon club met. Darwin was impressed with the odd characters at the club and their knowledge of pigeons. His close observation of the characteristics of particular breeds of pigeon allowed him to note the diversity amongst the different breeds:

Compare the English carrier and the short-faced tumbler, and see the wonderful difference in their beaks, entailing corresponding differences in their skulls. The carrier, especially the male bird, is also remarkable from the wonderful development of the carunculated skin about the head, and this is accompanied by greatly elongated eyelids, very large external orifices to the nostrils, and a wide gape of mouth.[28]

Breeding certain colours and other traits involves the genetic unit, the chromosome, and its behaviour during meiosis, when genes are exchanged and new DNA sequences are formed. Colour inheritance is a paint palette; a fascinating glimpse into the world of genetics, a dabble in the gene pool of DNA. It is also an entry point into the world and mind of pigeon breeders. 'Morph' is the word used by scientists to describe an inherited physical feature. For birds, an important morph is its feather colour. We know, by casual observation, that pigeons are polymorphs. Rock pigeons in the wild were of only one colour morph: blue-black and grey. They were captured, and people bred them. Over time, this breeding produced a number of different

Pouter, Fantail, Dragoon and Blondinette. Cigarette cards issued by Ogden's Cigarettes, 1904.

colour types (polymorphs), which extend to more than 28 different colour morphs. Beautiful descriptive terms are applied to their feather colouring. Words such as 'spread' (meaning the bird has one dark colour over its body), 'bars' (stripes on each of its lower wings), 'chequer' (the wings have checks of light and dark, similar to a draughtsboard), and 'pied' (markings of two or more colours) are reminiscent of dance classes and board games, rather than of feather pigment.

In addition to colour, patterns play a role in the field of genetics. There is Grizzle (a mixture of white with blue, dominant red and their dilutes), Opal (occurring in barred and chequered patterns, where the blue of the wing appears bleached to a much lighter shade), Mosaic (patches of different colours; more common in the male, so indicates a sexual difference), and the Spangling or Lacing (also known as stencilling, where silvery-white or bronze spots are superimposed on the chequered pattern).[29]

The three main colour pigments are black, brown and red. These are all melanins and occur in evenly spread granules.

German
cigarette cards.

With the colour blue, the black melanin granules are clumped together in the lighter areas, but in the darker regions, such as wing bars and/or tail bars, they are close together, not in a clump. These four intense colours, black, brown, red and blue, have corresponding dilutes. The pigment in the dilutes is sparsely distributed, which leads to the appearance of a different colour. Black corresponds to dun, blue to silver, brown to khaki and red to yellow. Whites have an absence of pigment granules.

The pigment blue broadens one's understanding of the complexities of genetics. Blue is the colour of the wild Blue Rock Pigeon, *Columba livia*. The colour blue is important because all colours are said to be either dominant or recessive according to their genetic behaviour in reference to the colour blue. There are four sub-varieties of blue pigeon: Black Chequered (T-Pattern), Blue Chequered, Blue-Barred and Blue-Barless. The Blue-Barless is a bit of a misnomer; although its wings do not feature bars, the tail feathers do.[30]

Silver is the corresponding dilute of blue, and is made up of black pigment. These colour granules are more sparsely arranged. If a silver hen is mated to a blue cock, the first generation will nearly always be blue.

The genetic calculations are complicated. Red, an intense colour, can be one of two types: dominant and recessive. If the colour is a solid red, seen in the Red Carneau and in the Red Self Tumbler, then this indicates a recessive type. The Mealy (Barred) or Red-Chequered Homers are the dominant type. Not all Reds can be categorized in this way; the only sure way of knowing whether they are recessive or dominant is by breeding from them.

Genetics also play a role in eye colour; for example, pearl eye is the lowest grade of iris pigmentation. The granules are colourless and are recessive to orange and yellow colour. If a pigeon has what is termed 'Pink Eye', this indicates an absence of pigment on the choroid and on the inner surface of the iris; these birds are visually impaired.

Some pigeon fanciers do not introduce outside blood into their inbred line of pigeons, in case the offspring exhibit an un-wanted characteristic that can take years to breed out in the line. Others broaden the genetic base, for sometimes the new genes will produce a superior bird, which the pure line was unable to do. Breeding involves both genetics and luck. Most breeders do not rely solely on blood lines, knowing that each pigeon needs to be assessed for its strengths, and knowing that there may come a time for new blood to be introduced into the mix.

> There are no pedigree systems of the pigeons; and perhaps it is just as well. Just as a champion may be descended from a mongrel, a bird of poor type may have descended from champions.[31]

The range of 'fancy' pigeons and doves is extraordinary. From oriental fantails, to odd-looking barbary pigeons, from the aerial twists of the tumblers, to the movements of the rollers, these birds defy general classification.

Eaton's *Treatise on the Almond Tumbler* (1851) addresses the temptation of becoming a pigeon fancier:

> If you have never thought before, and the perfections or imperfections of the fine properties of the Almond Tumbler cause you to begin thinking, the Fancy will be a blessing to you, for you cannot think hard or deeply on the Almond Tumbler without thinking on more impor-tant matters, which may lead to the salvation of your soul . . . then 'Should you', he says, 'give up attending the

THE "BOY'S OWN PAPER"]   George & Co., Nottingham.   [36, Paternoster Row.

OUR FANCY PIGEONS.
[Drawn for the "Boy's Own Paper" by A. F. LYDON.]

1. Black mottled short-faced Tumbler. 2. Red long-faced Tumbler. 3. Beard Tumbler. 4. Almond Tumbler. 5. Rushian Pigeon.
6. Fantail. 7. Priest. 8. Magpie. 9. Jacobin. 10. Baldhead. 11. Turbit. 12. Nun. 13. Dove. 14. English Owl. 15. Blondinette.
16. Turbiteen. 17. Trumpeter. 18. Swallow. 19. White-spot Pigeon. 20. Dragon. 21. Antwerp. 22. Runt. 23. Carrier.
24. Pouter. 25. Norwich Cropper. 26. Nun. 27. Yellow Spot. 28. Shield. 29. Full Back. 30. Homer. 31. Archangel. 32. Swift.
33. Trganica or Modena. 36. Hyacinth.

A. F. Lydon, *Fancy Pigeon Breeds*, engraving from the *Boy's Own Paper*.

house of God through your hobby for pigeons, give your pigeons up at once.'[32]

Fancy pigeons all descend from their common ancestor, the rock pigeon, *Columba livia*. Due to genetic plasticity, genetic mutations reveal amazing variation in shapes and sizes. These mutations have created feathered feet, unusual beaks, large crests

Columbia Livia, from *The Birds of Great Britain* by John Gould, vol. IV (London, 1873).

and bizarre flight displays. The Jacobin breed, popular with Queen Victoria, is a result of 500 years of breeding a mutation. The pigeon has a 'hood' of feathers which is so close to the head that at times visibility is restricted; sometimes the feathered hood has to be trimmed. Other fancy breeds, such as the Oriental Frill, have little beaks. This makes feeding their young next to impossible. The Frill Backs have feathers which curl. Due to their shape, these feathers are not water-repellent, and do not provide good insulation, hence there is heat loss. Rollers and tumblers are bred for their aerial acrobatics. They are impressive to watch, but, like the Oriental Frill and the Frill Backs (as well as other breeds), they are unsuitable for the wild. Pigeons need to be able to feed their young, keep warm and dry and not attract predators. Even though we may be amazed at the variety of the pigeons, and aghast at how little some of these fancy breeds resemble the common pigeon, it is humbling to note that when a pigeon mates with a pigeon of a different breed, in just a few generations the pigeons are back to the basic *Columba livia* – the rock pigeon. These mutations are, in a sense, only skin deep.

PIGEON INTELLIGENCE

How smart is a pigeon? People refer to them as 'dumb' or 'stupid', perhaps basing their findings on the pigeons sticking close by their feet in the busy cities, but is this so?

The size of the brain is not the issue; recent discoveries of the way a bird's brain processes information now rule out the 'size of the brain = intelligence' argument.

Brains of birds, unlike brains of mammals, do not have a neo-cortex (which is the highly developed outer section of the brain in mammals). Bird intelligence is found in the large amount of

The Jacobine Pidgeon. E. Albin Del. 1737.

tissue in another area of the brain, the paleocortex.[33] In 2005 this acceptance of bird intelligence was played out in the academic/scientific arena at an international consortium of bird brain experts. An announcement was made that the naming of the bird brain components was to be changed in recognition of new evidence that birds process information in much the same manner as mammals, but from a different region of the brain.[34] Social cognition, social awareness and animals' intelligence are now being reviewed and re-assessed. In the past, many scientists, biologists, zoologists and ethnologists were reluctant to view animal behaviour as an indicator of 'intelligence'; instead, such behaviour was categorized as 'instinctive', part of their evolutionary progress.[35]

It was winter . . . and no one wants to eat an ice cream in the winter so the guy who owned the shop had put all the seeds and popcorn on top of the fridges. As I walked by the shop, I saw a pigeon on the fridge pushing along bags of sunflower seeds with its beak. It was trying to get them to the edge of the fridge and push them down. When I looked down, there was another pigeon opening the seed

PIGEON CRAVATE FRANÇAIS.

Columba turbita Gallica.

PI. 18.

Pierrs Boitard and M. Corbie, 'Pigeon cravate Français, *Columba turbita Gallica*', from *Les Pigeons de volière et de Colombier* (Paris, 1824).

bags and eating . . . There was organized crime taking place right in front of my eyes![36]

Pigeons are one of the most intelligent birds; they are one of only six species, and the only non-mammal, to pass the 'mirror test' of being able to recognize their own reflection. Studies by Herrnstein and Loveland demonstrated that pigeons could differentiate between photographs, identifying categories such as 'tree' and 'fish'.[37] Research by Donald Blough uncovered the ability of pigeons to recognize the 26 letters of the English alphabet.[38] Blough devised a three-choice discrimination task in which three white Carneaux pigeons learned to distinguish each letter of the alphabet from all other letters. On the monitor screen three response keys were displayed; the pigeon would be rewarded for pecking at the 'target' letter behind a response key on four successive daily sessions. When the response was correct, the three letters stood out, then disappeared from the screen, and the bird was rewarded with three-second access to seed in the feeder. If, however, one of the non-target keys was pecked, the letters disappeared, then the target letter reappeared on the same key, with black blocks replacing the non-target letters. After each target letter was used for four sessions, a new target letter replaced it. The data, in this case the errors, was arranged in hierarchical clusters and as a two-dimensional representation. Letters that look similar, such as 'u' and 'v', scored a high rate of error (34 per cent). Blough hypothesizes about the universality of pattern (or, in this case, 'letter') recognition: 'The results resembled those generated from similarity judgments by humans, suggesting cross-task and cross-species generality in processes of letter discrimination.'[39]

In studies by a team at Keio University, Japan, pigeons have been credited with similar levels of intelligence to those found in

Jasmine, a white-headed pigeon.

a three-year-old child. Each pigeon test subject was shown live footage of itself, and then there was a delay of several seconds. Amazingly, the birds were able to tell the difference between the live video images and the previously recorded images. Professor Shigeru Watanabe said: 'The pigeon could discriminate the present self-image and the recorded self-image of the past with a few seconds delay, which means that the pigeon has self-cognitive abilities.'[40]

Previous research by the Keio University team demonstrated that pigeons were able to differentiate between the paintings of Picasso and those of Monet.[41] The first experiment, to test if pigeons could discriminate between photographs or videos of paintings by Monet and those of Picasso, involved eight pigeons, divided into two groups.[42] When shown a Picasso, pigeons would obtain food by pecking, but when the artwork was by Monet, pecking had no effect. Eventually the pigeons only pecked when shown a Picasso. In the first experiment, the first test used monochromatic pictures so that a difference in colour could not be a clue for discrimination. In the second test, the paintings were presented slightly out of focus, to examine the role of contour (which is sharper in Picasso's work). The results indicted that sharpness of edges did not strongly control discrimination. In the third test, three of the pictures were reversed, and another three seen upside down. This decreased recognition of Monet's work, but not of Picasso's:

> The present tests with rotated paintings suggest that this distortion disrupts control when the original stimulus represents a real object (as in Monet's paintings), but less disruption is produced when the stimulus has a weaker relation with the real world (as in Picasso's paintings).[43]

The fourth test involved discrimination between other works by Monet and Picasso, as well as paintings by other pre-Impressionists and Impressionists (Cézanne, Renoir and Delacroix) and abstract painters (Braque and Matisse). This, of course, does not mean that the pigeon indicates which he prefers; as far as the researchers can tell, this plays no part; it is more to do with observation, which involves, in all tests bar the first, colour, as well as thickness of brushstroke and the recognition of objects in the paintings. Although Impressionism aims to record fleeting 'impressions', especially of natural light, it does not set out to represent or to record reality, a task more suited to photography. Having said this, it appears that pigeons were able to discriminate between paintings with recognizable objects

'Colombar à queue Pointue', *Columba oxyura*. Engraving by César Macret after Madame Knip, from her *Les Pigeons* (Paris, 1811).

within them and those without (or with less identifiable items). In an earlier study, Herrnstein and Loveland were able to demonstrate pigeons' ability to discriminate between a photograph and the actual object. Now we are closer to understanding how pigeons 'see' their world. If paintings represent a three-dimensional world, then 'we can presume that it can see a painting as a representation of a three-dimensional world'.[44]

Porter and Neuringer studied pigeons' ability to learn to discriminate between complex musical sequences, as well as to link composers to others of the same era, similar to the Keio University's painting study.[45] In the first experiment, two white Carneaux pigeons were exposed to a one-minute excerpt from a Bach prelude, which was continually repeated, and a one-minute excerpt from Paul Hindemith's Sonata for viola, Op. 25 No. 1, which was also continually repeated. The range of intervals varied from 5 seconds to 3 minutes. When the Bach excerpt was played, if the pigeon pecked the left key, the pigeon received some seed; when the Hindemith piece was played, food was not available (that is, the action was not reinforced). Both birds learned to discriminate between Bach and Hindemith (more than 80 per cent were correct responses). In the second experiment, which was to confirm and extend the findings from the first, longer musical pieces were used. The time frame varied from 1 minute to over 20 minutes. Pigeons used were of three different breeds (two White Carneaux, a Schietti Modena and two Silver Kings), as a way to extend the generality of the findings. The music played was some excerpts from Bach, and Stravinsky's *Rite of Spring*. Two response discs were used; the left being the one to be pecked when Bach was played, the right for Stravinsky. Both were reinforced with seed if the responses were correct (in this experiment, more than 70 per cent of responses were correct). The findings confirmed and extended those from the first experiment. There was a third experiment to test if pigeons could respond to categories of music. Four pigeons used in the second experiment were exposed to a range of music they had not heard before. Excerpts from Buxtehude, Vivaldi and Scarlatti (all composed before 1750 and similar to Bach) were played, as well as music composed after 1900: Elliott Carter, Walter Piston and another piece by Stravinsky (the *Firebird Suite*), using a variety of instruments.[46] The pigeons responded to the type of music (that is, Bach or baroque style, left key; contemporary or Stravinsky style, right key) rather than to the particular musical instrument being played. In order to compare pigeons with people, a group of seven college students was put through similar tests.

The results were revealing; both the pigeons and the humans responded similarly, with one exception: their responses to Vivaldi. All four pigeons differed in the same way, consistently pecking at the 'Stravinsky' key (that is, contemporary) rather than at the 'Bach' key. With the exception of the piece by Vivaldi, the pigeons and the human group responded similarly to the categorization of musical stimuli: 'Therefore the pigeon's response to complex auditory events may be more like the human's than is often assumed.'[47]

Porter and Neuringer's research concentrated on discrimination and categorization; it did not address music preference. Do pigeons display likes and dislikes for particular pieces of music? Using anecdotal evidence of an earlier period, Boria Sax relates this story:

Bigley tells of a pigeon in the neighbourhood of a young lady who played brilliantly on the harpsichord; the pigeon did not greatly care about her playing, except when she played the song of 'Spera sì', from Handel's opera,

Admetus; then it would come and sit by the window, testifying pleasure; when the song was over, it would fly back to its dovecote, for it had not learned the art of clapping wings for an encore.[48]

NAVIGATIONAL ABILITIES

Darwin said little about pigeons' homing abilities. In a sense, Darwin was on the cusp of a new era, that of pigeon racing. It wasn't until 1858, when 110 pigeons from Antwerp were released from London Bridge, in order to fly 'home', that this ability started to be spoken about and to cause excitement. As Wynne notes, in 1858 Darwin was on the Isle of Wight, compiling what was to become *On the Origin of Species*;[49] either news of the birds' flight came too late to be included in his work, or the event went unnoticed by a preoccupied Darwin.

Pigeons' navigational abilities are exceptional. There are a number of hypotheses to explain homing in pigeons, none conclusive. One, sun navigation, proposed by Matthews, suggests that pigeons

> extrapolate a short portion of the sun's arc, measured at the displaced position, to the noon altitude and compare it with the altitude last seen at home for latitudinal displacement. If the noon altitude observed is lower than that remembered from home the bird would be north of home. If the noon altitude observed is higher than that of home the bird would be south of home.[50]

However, the use of a variety of experiments, including clock-shift experiments and sun-occlusion experiments, have demonstrated that the sun is not used for navigational purposes by pigeons.

Racing pigeons.

A number of arguments were levelled against the acceptance of Matthews's hypothesis, the first being that the sun-arc hypothesis would require the pigeon to measure changes in azimuth. At present, there is no evidence to suggest that a bird in flight can do this. A second reason is that there is no evidence that a pigeon has a rigidly stable chronometer that keeps home time.

Another factor is vision; although pigeons do have remarkable vision, scientists doubt that they possess the vision needed for sun navigation. So, if sun navigation is not the whole answer, what is?

Perhaps part of the answer lies within non-visual clues. A theory raised by Papi and his co-workers concerns the pigeons' use of olfactory navigation. They suggest that pigeons create an olfactory or scent map, cataloguing smells from birth. Different smells alert them to varied directions: sea, forest and cities. In their early life, they associate odours with the direction that the odours come from. When they are being moved from an area (for example, being transported to a race), they store up the odours, and reverse them on the return flight for the direction of home. Experiments have not been conclusive, so olfactory navigation is still part of the discussion concerning pigeon homing skills. Some scientists raise considerable doubts about the importance of olfactory cues.

Another theory, that of magnetic cues, suggests that pigeons navigate by using a grid formed by the magnetic and geographic poles, which could be used for navigational purposes. The geomagnetic field could be drawn on for orientation, and possibly for navigation. In the early 1970s several experiments concerning magnetic compass orientation were successfully carried out on pigeons. These experiments, using bar magnets, or coils and batteries, showed that a magnetic field could be produced around the pigeon. As they became disorientated, the results seemed to indicate that the pigeons did not switch between their magnetic compass and their sun compass; instead, the systems seemed to interact.[51] The magnetic sensitivity of the pigeon appeared to be high. The magnetic fields of the earth can be demonstrated to have some bearing on their navigational skills. There certainly does appear to be strong support and evidence to support the claim that pigeon flight is affected by the earth's magnetic field, but how do pigeons sense these magnetic cues?

Recent research has found that pigeons, along with other creatures that have heightened homing abilities, have clusters of tiny ion crystals, magnetite, located in the nerve endings of the upper beak. These ions are highly sensitive to magnetic fields. The ions lie in clusters on different axes, giving the pigeon three-dimensional information about the earth's magnetic field. This means that the pigeon has magnetic sense, due to a built-in tracking device that plots its course home and that senses changes in the magnetic field.

It seems that how pigeons 'home' comes down to the pigeon having two compasses, the sun compass and the magnetic compass, each compass operating quite differently.[52] Numerous experiments have been conducted to suggest and to confirm that pigeons do draw on these compasses when homing. While it has been established that these compasses are important in homing flights, there are still questions that remain unanswered. Are pigeons using other factors to determine homing flights? They see ultraviolet light, they detect changes in pressure, they hear infrasound, and are highly skilled in spatial intelligence.

Pigeons appear to have a better grasp than humans at recognizing when objects have been rotated. Tests have shown that pigeons are able to recognize shapes, and even when the shape is partly obscured, the pigeon is still able to recognize the outline. This recognition of shapes and outlines appears to be crucial in their navigational abilities. Outlines of buildings and highways guide them home, and when off track other systems kick in. Jonathan Balcombe suggests that this is due to their 'bird's eye' view of the world; they are able to recognize familiar landmarks from different angles due to observation while flying.[53] Other research supports this, adding that pigeons seem to use their

PIGEON PATU LIMOUSIN.

Columba Lemovicensis pedibus plumosis.

PL. 3.

knowledge of human transport routes to aid them in their navigation, even turning at highway junctions.[54] This would be advantageous, for it would free the pigeons to observe the remainder of their airspace, freeing them to note the early approach of predators. Researchers suggest that this highlights both the pigeons' intelligence and their flexibility. No one would question the sophistication of their homing abilities; but when one realizes that the pigeon uses this skill when it is in unfamiliar territory, perhaps switching to following familiar routes when they know the area, then this is certainly an example of adaptability and flexibility. Memory also plays a part, with aerial road maps, or mental maps, being part of their navigational equipment, perhaps alongside olfactory clues.

When we consider all the theories about the homing abilities of pigeons, perhaps we need to ask the question: why does this interest us so much? Compasses indicate direction, but not goals. Is there a deeper longing in our own hearts which prompts us to wonder at the homing ability of the humble pigeon? Jon Carroll wrote about this yearning when recording an experiment in homing where the pigeons had been raised in a moveable coop; a trailer on a truck. The main focus of the experiment was to note what would happen to the flight path when 'home' was moved: 'home' was still the same, but its location had changed, or moved. The pigeons found their home; 'the idea of "home" . . . is more powerful than the idea of "place".'[55]

> [Pigeons] know that home is not necessarily a single point on the planet. Home is where the heart is, where the food is; home is the wide place in the road where the perch is. Home is where you go when you go home.
>
> This happens to a lot of us, does it not? They keep moving home on us. We think we know where it is, and then the people who made it home move, or die, or go crazy . . . And we have to know where home is anyway. That is our challenge. We have to understand that it is not one specific spot on the globe. Science has now taught us that we are none of us homeless . . . Not by the stars or the sun or the fluctuations in the magnetic field, but by something else – we know.[56]

Could this be the reason for naming them 'homing' pigeons? Pigeon racers have an inkling of what constitutes 'home'. For years, many pigeon racers have separated the racers from their mates several days before a race, so that they will rush home to be reunited. They will find 'home' wherever it may be, fixed or in a new location, drawn by the attraction of their mate. Perhaps that old saying is true; home is where the heart (or mate) is.

2 Heaven-sent: Religion and Mythology

The dove has some excellent traits
Which we ought to keep in mind.
Seven attributes of her nature
Deserve foremost consideration:
She has no bitter bile in her,
And we too should be humble and peace-loving.
She doesn't live by thievery,
And we too should renounce robbery.
She abstains from worms and lives on seed,
Just as we have need of Christ's precepts.
She acts like a mother with other birds,
As each of us should treat our fellow man.
Her cry is like a lament and sorrowful,
As befits us when we have done wrong.
In the water she is wary of the hawk's arrival.
As the Bible tells us to be of the Devil's clutches.
She makes her nest in a hole in solid rock.
And in Christ's mercy exists our firmest hope.[1]

The paradox continues into the realm of religion and mythology. Pigeons have been held in high regard in religion and religious ritual through the centuries; in some instances they have been singled out as the only bird suitable to offer as a sacrifice (that is, the only one pleasing to God). Their role in religious practice has spanned different religions and cultures.

From early beginnings, the dove has been included in several creation myths. The Andamanese myth spoke of their importance, for Lady Dove was the wife of the first human, Tomo.[2] The mythical pre-Grecian goddess, Eurynome, assumed the form of a dove and laid the universal egg.[3]

In African mythology, the dove represents love and mutual help. For the Yoruba people, the dove symbolizes prosperity and honour. In one of the Yoruba's myths, the dove, a wild bird, was lamenting that she had no children. The king of the Odu deities, Eji Ogbe, heard the lament and promised her children if she followed his advice. She was to build her nest next to his house (that is, become domesticated) and she would have young. The dove moved the site of her nest, and she did indeed have young. Eji Ogbe decreed that she would have two eggs each time (which is the laying practice of doves), becoming the mother of twins.[4] In Africa pigeons and doves are perceived as key messenger birds.

In Aboriginal (or indigenous Australian) Dreamtime[5] pigeons have key roles in several legends. One of these, concerning Marnpi, the bronze-winged pigeon from Baratta, explains the origins of the rich mineral deposits in the area around the township of Broken Hill. The wounded pigeon flew to the quartz outcrops of Broken Hill. Its dropped feathers formed the gold, silver and shiny rocks, and its blood the white rusty rocks (the ore) at Broken Hill. The pigeon's track is marked by gold and silver mines.[6]

In the Fertile Crescent (a section of fertile land in the Middle East where the Sumerian, Babylonian, Assyrian, Phoenician and Hebrew civilizations thrived), their use in sacrifice in Mesopotamian and Hittite rituals was common; it was as though these sacrifices were directed upwards, toward the deities being worshipped. Even the saying 'May my headache fly like a dove to the west' was connected with this image of sacrifice.[7]

Doves were kept, and domesticated, in Egypt from at least 3000 BC. In Egypt, during the reign of Rameses III, more than 57,000 pigeons were sacrificed to the god Ammon at Thebes in the twelfth century BC.[8] Dove images have been found on bas-reliefs and in tombs. On one Egyptian bas-relief a coronation procession is depicted in which birds are being released from cages by priests.[9] In the annals of Tuthmosis III (fifteenth century BC), reference is made to '258 pairs of pigeons and 5,237 pigeons of another kind'.[10] They continued to form a part of key rituals for the Mesopotamians and the Hittites. The goddess Anath counted doves as one of her favourite animals. As cultivation of pigeons took hold in Egypt, devices were constructed in order to prevent pigeons from leaving the dovecotes. One method to stop their departure was the use of an ancient Egyptian charm in the form of a bat's head.[11]

According to the Greek writers Xenophon, Ctesias and Lucian, the Achaemenid Persians worshipped pigeons and doves, or were at least mindful and protective of them, seeing them as being of a divine nature. Xenophon (c. 428–c. 355 BC) refers to the Persians' regard for them (*Anabasis* 1.6).[12] Latin writers also knew how the Syrians esteemed them; Tibullus wrote: 'Why need I tell how the sacred pigeon flutters unmolested about the numerous cities of Syrian Palestine?'[13] In Syria it was taboo to kill and consume a dove, due to the popular belief that the dove was a symbol of the soul and a bearer of the soul of the dead.[14] The dove was also

Earrings,
c. 200–100 BC,
Greek, gold
with enamel
and a garnet.

59

connected to the Syrian fertility goddess, Atargatis, who had a dove on the top of her sceptre.

Doves became associated with sexuality, love and fidelity. This association correlates with the way the dove has been perceived in some aspects of religion and mythology. In Greek mythology, Aphrodite, the goddess of love, was born from an egg brooded by a dove. The dove is the symbol of Venus, the Roman goddess of love. Doves were viewed as her messengers or representatives, vehicles of love and passion. Sometimes Venus is depicted in a chariot drawn by two doves. Love and passion as attributes of the dove were viewed in a similar manner in the Middle East, where the dove embodied sexuality through the goddesses Astarte and Isis. And yet here we note another seeming paradox: on the one hand the dove represents sexuality and passion, and on the other she is viewed as a symbol of motherhood and the maternal instinct. Of course, passion and motherhood are not mutually exclusive, but there are times when these qualities are viewed as opposites. The dove is also a simile for fidelity, perhaps not so readily linked with Venus, whose attributes of passion and sexuality are better known. Amongst young females, the dove represented purity and innocence; statues of doves have been found adorning Greek tombstones of young girls from the fourth and fifth centuries BC.

Zeus was fed ambrosia by a flock of doves, and as a way of thanking them he set them in the sky where they became the starry Pleiades.[15] Others say that the doves fed him when he was a baby, in a cave in Crete.[16] As well as the starry Pleiades, there is another constellation, Columba, set in the heavens in memory of a heroic act performed by a dove. Phineus had given the Argonauts good advice as they set out on their journey. When their boat approached the Symplegades, the rocks appeared to close in. Near the entrance, the Argonauts released a white dove. They had been told that any living thing that passed through the Symplegades would mean that the rocks would never move again. The white dove, aided by Athene, flew at great speed through the entrance. The rocks crashed together, but the bird survived, losing a few feathers. As the cliffs went backwards, the Argo began to sail between the rocks and completed their journey through the Sympleglades. When the rocks realized that they had been tricked, they crashed together for the last time. Since then they have been known as the Dardanelles, guarding the Bosphorus, the passage between the Aegean Sea and the Black Sea. The dove returned to the ship, and Athene placed her amongst the stars as the constellation Columba. The constellation, also known as Columba Noae, Noah's Dove, depicts a dove holding an olive branch.

At Dodona in Epirus, the site of an ancient oracle dedicated to Zeus, the prophecies were delivered by the rustling of leaves in a sacred oak, and then interpreted by the priests. The priestesses at the shrine were known as 'doves'. The cooing of pigeons were seen as additional signs, messages from the gods. According to another legend there were two black pigeons residing in Thebes; one flew to Libya, the other to Dodona. Here the oracle of Jupiter was established, and the pigeons in the area were thereby accorded sacred status.[17] The sacred site of Dodona became associated with the gift of prophecy. Many people sought guidance from the oracle of Dodona, including Alexander the Great. The temple birds were regarded as sacred; it was forbidden to kill them except for the purpose of sacrifice.

Birds were accorded mysterious powers in Biblical times and earlier, for they could soar up towards the dwelling of God (or the gods). They were regarded as symbols of freedom. Even their Latin name attests to this: *aves* (Latin for 'bird') is perhaps

a combination of *a* and *via*, 'without road or pathway'.[18] The mysterious nature of the bird is reflected in 'when a bird flies through the air, no evidence of its passage is found' (Wisdom of Solomon 5:11).

Pigeons and doves are mentioned in the Bible more than any other bird.[19] One writer holds that 'the dove is indisputably the most important bird in the Bible'.[20] Ecclesiastes 10:20 is an early reference to a carrier pigeon relaying a message, and to the fanciful idea that birds will tell of the gossip they hear: 'Do not curse the king . . . for a bird of the air may carry your voice, or some winged creature tell the matter.' One book of the Bible has 'dove' as its title: 'Jonah' (yônah) means 'dove'. Perhaps the name indicates something about Jonah's character, which we may interpret from the reference to Ephraim – 'Ephraim has become like a dove, silly and without sense' (Hosea 7:11) – for Jonah is 'without sense' during key moments in his life.

The well-known story of Noah's Ark includes a dove being sent out to see if it can land. Perhaps the dove was actually a homing pigeon, as it returned to the ark twice. Several myths and legends accompany this story, including an explanation for the lack of a gall bladder in the anatomy of the pigeon. Apparently when the pigeon/dove left the ark, it was so overcome by grief at what had happened to the earth that its gall bladder burst.[21] Since that day, they have been non-gallinaceous (minus a gall bladder). No particular animal or bird is named as the one chosen to be the burnt offering at the conclusion of the story, but it is highly likely to have been a pigeon or dove.

Noah Releasing the Dove, mosaic, basilica of San Marco, Venice, 13th century.

The story of the Flood inspired Dryden to write *To Her Grace of Ormond*, which describes the return of the dove to the Ark:

> As when the dove returning bore the mark
> Of Earth restor'd to the long lab'ring ark,
> The relics of mankind, secure of rest,
> Oped every window to receive the guest,
> And the fair bearer of the message bless'd.

The account of the Flood has generated modern and ancient stories; Stefan Zweig's *Legend of the Third Dove* is a modern Midrash. It explores the story of the third dove that was released by Noah. In the biblical text it appears that the same dove was sent out three times, but in Zweig's narrative, three different doves are sent. The third dove forgets its mission and settles down in the woods, able to survive by virtue of being one of the original inhabitants of the Ark. After many years its peace is disturbed by another Flood of Destruction; this time the Flood is war, and fire consumes the earth. The dove flies off, unable to find rest, and unable to find its protector. For Zweig, the dove's fear is an allegory for the present state of the world; the dove becomes a symbol of peace.[22] There have been a number of children's books which tell the story of the Flood from different perspectives; from the point of view of Mrs Noah, or from a feminist perspective, leaving Noah out of the picture in *Norah's Ark*.[23] Nicholas Allan's *The Dove*[24] is about co-existence; a hermit loves his quiet, peaceful island and lifestyle until he receives an unwelcome visitor, the dove from the Ark. Eventually, after many incidents, he is able to live happily with the new resident.

The role of the dove in the story of Noah has bestowed upon it the characteristics of loyalty and trustworthiness. According to an Irish myth, the dove received the raven's sheen, because it had been obedient, unlike the raven, and hence was rewarded for its obedience.[25] In the Arabian version of the Flood narrative, Wilkinson writes:

> On its second visit to the ark, the red appearance of its feet proved that the red mud on which it had walked was already freed from the waters; and to record the event, Noah prayed that the feet of these birds might for ever continue of that colour, which marks them to the present day.[26]

In the Sumerian saga the *Epic of Gilgamesh*,[27] the narrative of the Flood, or the Deluge, is quite different. On the seventh day a dove is released, but returns when it is unable to land, due to the water level. Later a swallow is cast out from the ark, followed by a raven, so in this account of the flood, the dove is given a minor part to play. In another section, Enkidu tells Gilgamesh about the dream he had the night before. In the dream, Enkidu says that he was turned into a dove, and 'He trussed my limbs like a bird's.'[28]

The Aztecs had their own account of a great flood. Most of the humans were wiped out; only two survived, a man named Coxcoxtli and a woman named Xochiquetzal, who had managed to escape in a boat. They found dry land on top of a mountain, settled there and raised a large family. The gift of languages was given to them by a dove. This was a mixed blessing; there were so many languages that the children did not understand one another.[29]

In the Bible, three birds are mentioned as being suitable (and therefore permitted) for consumption: the quail, the dove and the turtledove. In ancient Israel pigeons were an integral component of the Levitical sacrificial system, particularly in purification offerings. Pigeons were used before this by Abraham (Genesis 15:9), where both turtledoves and a young pigeon were sacrificed. Perhaps this is one of the reasons why, in later texts, the sacrificial birds were restricted to turtledoves and pigeons (Leviticus 5:11, 12:8). Another reason is almost certainly because they were not included in the list of 'unclean' birds (Leviticus 5:2). Pigeons and doves eat seeds, fruits and greens, meaning they were considered clean by the Hebrews, and were therefore suitable for eating and for sacrifice.[30] The 'young' pigeon is included in both the burnt offering and the purification offering. Levi suggests that both the dove and the turtledove were included because the turtledove was migratory, and therefore unavailable in every season, so the pigeon was a necessary alternative.[31] Levi also points out that sacrificial sites were often in high places; pigeons love to roost on cliffs, buildings and other 'high places', so were easy to obtain in these regions. Pigeons were offerings for the purification of Nazarites, for lepers and for mothers after childbirth.

Bernard Lazare suggests another reason for the choice of the dove:

Look in the literature, there is no bird so persecuted as the Dove: nevertheless it was she that God chose to be sacrificed on his altar. God said: 'Offer me in holocaust not those who persecute but those who are persecuted.'[32]

Turtledoves or pigeons provided a means of sacrifice for the poor. Unlike the regulation for sacrificial animals, there was no requirement that the birds be without blemish or that they were required to be male. Of course, feathers make it hard to detect blemishes or sex. Due to their plentiful numbers, it would be assumed that if a bird were blemished, the sacrificer could easily substitute another in its place. In the Gospel of Luke, Mary and Joseph provided the doves (or pigeons) necessary for the purification offering after the birth of Jesus. The addition of birds to the list of animals suitable for sacrifice allowed all, rich and poor, to participate in this religious ritual.[33]

Were these birds domesticated? Their frequent use implies that they were: 'Who are they that fly like a cloud, and like doves to their windows?' (Isaiah 60:8) suggests that doves were being bred in captivity, perhaps in an early version of a dovecote. In the Gospel of John, Jesus enters the Temple and singles out the bird-sellers. The doves had been trapped and snared in nets to provide the sacrifice in the temple, as well as being for general consumption. 'As they go, I will cast my net over them' (Hosea 7:12) is a reference to the decoy dove, or a 'stool pigeon'. These decoys, used to trap others of their kind for food, were sometimes blinded by a red-hot needle[34] before being tied to a stake and placed in an open area where others of its kind would fly overhead. It would be crouching in fear and, hearing the cries of its own kind, it too would call out, hoping to join them. The flock overhead would fly down, enabling the fowler to throw out his net and catch them.

There have been discoveries of large columbaria at Maresha and elsewhere, which suggests that the raising of pigeons domestically, or in a controlled environment, has been going on for a long time, perhaps related to the time and task of raising other domestic fowl, such as chickens. Cages were probably used, and there is evidence to suggest that the rock pigeon was one of the first, and more than likely the most common, of caged pet birds.[35]

In Palestinian caves bird relics are rare, and tend to be limited to the caves of Zuttiyeh and Umm Qatafah.[36] Excavation of shrines to Astarte have revealed figures of doves on their roofs.

In Israel evidence of bird bones has been found at Tell Jemmeh supporting the theory that pigeons and doves were domesticated here.[37] The bones found at the Tell were divided into six categories, of which the ground-bird group included pigeons and doves.[38] During the Middle Bronze and Late Bronze Ages the bones of water birds appeared seven times as frequently as those of the ground birds.[39] Changes occurred after the beginning of the Iron Age, when ground birds were one and a half times more frequent than water birds.[40] Evidence found in Jerusalem, dated to the Iron Age, suggests that both wild and domestic birds were consumed by the inhabitants.[41] The consumption of wild fowl meant that the inhabitants were relying on people who were involved in the occupation of fowling.

In the Old Testament there are numerous references to pigeons and doves, from the psalmist praising the beauty of the dove's feathers as they shimmer in the sun – 'the wings of a dove covered with silver, its pinions with yellow gold' (Psalms 68:13) – to the lover being compared to a dove: 'His eyes are like doves beside springs of water' (Song of Solomon 5:12). The turtledove heralds the coming of spring: 'and the time of singing has come, and the voice of the turtledove is heard in our land' (Song of Solomon 2:12). This could be a reference to the migration of the turtledove in April, during the northern passage.[42] Mendelssohn's setting of Psalm 55:6 is well known: 'O, that I had wings like a dove! I would fly away and be at rest.'[43]

In 2 Kings 6:25 the cost of doves' dung is mentioned to highlight the exorbitant price items were fetching during a wartime siege. It may have been a reference to the bulbs of certain white meadow flowers, known as 'doves' dung' or 'doves' milk',[44] rather than actual dung. Biblical scholars do not agree on this, but it is worth noting that these meadow flowers have kept the Latin name *Ornithogallum* ('bird milk').[45]

Although pigeons and doves were highly regarded in religious circles, certain practices connected with them were not. In the Talmud it is written that 'flyers of pigeons are liars'.[46] There are several interpretations concerning this injunction. First, people who race pigeons are gamblers, therefore they are not credible witnesses (pigeon racing was common in Palestine around AD 200–220;[47] betting on racing pigeons was frowned upon). Second, this quotation recognizes the foul practice of snaring, or thieving, other people's pigeons.

In Christianity the dove is the most common symbol of the Holy Spirit, one of the Three Persons of the Trinity. At the Annunciation the angel Gabriel tells Mary that during her conception the Holy Spirit will overshadow her. In religious artwork of the Annunciation the Holy Spirit is usually depicted as a dove. In the Middle Ages it was sometimes suggested that Mary conceived through her ear (*conceptio per aurem*). Perhaps the clerics thought this happened through the whispers of the dove. Legend suggests that the dove was not only present at the Annunciation, but also at the Crucifixion:

> It is said that a dove perched in the neighbourhood of the Holy Cross when the Redeemer was expiring and, wailing its notes of sorrow, kept repeating the words 'Kyrie! Kyrie!' (meaning 'Lord have mercy!') to alleviate the agony of His dying moments.[48]

At the baptism of Jesus, the Holy Spirit is portrayed as a dove: 'I saw the Spirit descending from heaven like a dove, and it remained on him' (John 1:32).[49] One superstition – that if your pillow is stuffed with dove feathers, you will not die – stems from the fact that the dove symbolizes the Holy Spirit. One will be protected from death by being in its presence. One folklore tale

claims that the devil can change into any shape except that of the dove or the lamb, since the dove is the symbol of the Trinity and of purity, and the lamb is that of innocence and sacrifice.

In Roman catacombs doves represent the human soul. Pigeon lofts were built on top of large tombs. During the medieval era dovecotes were frequently erected alongside graveyards to assist the spirit as it left the body in the form of a dove.

In the early years of Christian persecution birds were one of the secret symbols that signified a Christian. Birds that flew were seen as a sign of the Crucifixion, for while in flight they made a sign of the cross with their opened wings. Doves, symbols of the Crucifixion but also of the Holy Spirit, were chalked on

White doves in flight.

walls, 'embroidered on kerchiefs and shawls [and] engraved on signet rings'.[50]

Perceiving the dove as a symbol of the divine continued. During the Middle Ages the dove became linked with the legend of King Arthur. In Malory's *Morte d'Arthur* a dove, carrying a gold censer in its beak, flies into the castle. The knights of the Round Table are immediately struck by this symbol of purity.[51]

Pewter church decoration, English, 18th century.

Church art and architecture also depict the dove. In early Christian churches, the pyx (a vessel hanging over the altar) was sometimes fashioned in the shape of a dove. Stained-glass windows feature doves in Bible stories, including those of Creation, Noah's Ark and the baptism of Jesus. Sometimes the dove is on its own, with seven rays radiating from it to seven stars (symbolic of the seven gifts of the Holy Spirit). In other art, usually works of hagiography, several saints and martyrs are portrayed with a dove nearby, representing the soul. These saints include St Agnes (with a dove bearing a ring), and St Gregory the Great (usually depicted as a figure absorbed in the act of writing, with a dove resting on his shoulder). St Columba (Latin for 'dove') is associated with the dove, as is St Kenelm, son of Cenwulf, King of Mercia. Kenelm's sister, Cwnedridra[52] persuaded her lover, who was Kenelm's tutor and guardian, to kill him in the forest of Clent, Worcestershire. The news of his death was relayed to Rome via a dove, which landed on the high altar at St Peter's, carrying a letter in its beak. Another version has a white dove with golden wings ascending to heaven after Kenelm is murdered.[53] These two variants of the legend highlight the significance of the tale, as well as the symbolism of the dove: one represents Kenelm's soul, the other is a heavenly messenger. Other saints are also associated with doves. When St Scholastica died, her soul, according to witnesses, ascended to heaven in the form of a dove. So, too, did the soul of the saintly abbot Spes. When St David was preaching to a large crowd at the gathering of the Synod of Llanddewi Brefi, people complained that they couldn't hear him. The ground on which he was standing became a small hill, and a white dove was seen settling on his shoulder as a sign of God's blessing and favour.[54]

One of the stories associated with St Francis of Assisi mentions his kindness to turtledoves. Francis saw a cage of turtledoves that

72

had been captured by a young man. Francis, feeling sorry for the caged birds, begged the man to let him have them: 'I pray that you will give them to me, these birds that are so gentle, which holy scripture compares to chaste, humble, and faithful souls'.[55] Francis took them back to the monastery and cared for them.

The dove also serves as a metaphor for the church. Hugh of St Victor wrote:

> The dove has two wings even as the Christian has two ways of life, the active and the contemplative. The blue feathers of the wings are thoughts of heaven; the uncertain shades of the body, the changing colours that recall an unquiet sea, symbolize the ocean of human passion in which the Church is sailing. Why are the dove's eyes this beautiful golden colour? Because yellow, the colour of ripe fruit, is the colour too of experience and maturity, and the yellow eyes of the dove are the looks full of wisdom which the Church casts on the future. The dove, moreover, has red feet, for the Church moves through the world with her feet in the blood of the martyrs.[56]

In *Henry IV, Part II*, the Earl of Westmoreland, when addressing the Archbishop of York, refers to his 'white investments figure innocence,/The dove and very blessed spirit of peace',[57] again associating doves with innocence and purity; here the clergy is to follow suit. There may be a hint of irony in the Earl's address.

Many show, or fancy, pigeons have names associated with Christianity: Monk, Nun, Capuchine (a friar of the Franciscan order), Priest, Saint and Archangel.

Angels are sometimes portrayed with the wings of a snow-white dove. As angels are often credited with the task of bearing souls to heaven, some believe the dove does the same. In the

Uniting Church logo.

Nun.   Barb.   Jacobine.

lyrics of the Cat Stevens song 'Oh Very Young', this is alluded to in the line: 'when you ride the great white bird into heaven'. The combination of wings, feathers, whiteness and innocence is striking. In Venice, on the first day of Holy Week, during the Palm Sunday Procession of the Guilds in the Piazza di San Marco, the Comb and Lantern Makers' Guild carry a cage of birds. The doves are released in the presence of the Doge.[58] Legend has it that the pigeons fly around the Square three times daily, in honour of the Trinity, and there is a belief that as long as the pigeons are present in the dome of San Marco the sea will never fully encroach upon the city.[59] Perhaps there are symbolic links between the beginning of Holy Week and the need for repentance and the yearning for innocence, purity and forgiveness, as well as a ritualized seeking of the presence of the Spirit, symbolized by the release of the doves.

In Italy a bread shaped like a dove and called Columba is traditionally eaten at Easter. It was first produced in the twelfth century to celebrate the victory of the Milanese army against the army of Emperor Frederick Barbarossa.

The dove continued to be viewed as a symbol of the Divine and as a harbinger of good news or hope. In 1504, during Hernán Cortés's first voyage to the Caribbean, the crew had become discouraged and they were dangerously mutinous.

Pigeons in the Piazza di San Marco, Venice, Italy.

Then, according to Cortés's record of the voyage, 'came a Dove flying to the shippe, being Good Friday at Sunsett; and sat him on the Shippe-top; wherat they were all comforted, and tooke it for a miracle and good token . . . and all gave heartie thanks to God, directing our course the way the Dove flew.'[60]

Doves were prominent in the Bestiaries of the Middle Ages. In *Physiologus*, one of the most popular and widely read books of the Middle Ages, pagan tales were imbued with Christian morals and mystical teaching. These stories occupied an important role in the Christian world for their Christianized symbolism became established in iconography, preaching and poetry. The anonymous author of *Physiologus* wrote of the chastity and fidelity of the turtledove, offering it as an example of the Christian life:

> Take note, therefore, all you souls of the faithful, how much chastity is found in a small bird. All you who bear the person of the turtle-dove in the visage of the soul, imitate her chastity. For such is the holy church which, after seeing her mate crucified and resurrected on the third day and ascended into heaven, does not take another mate but longs for him and awaits him enduring in love and charity until death.[61]

In Section L, 'On the Doves', the author deciphers the meaning of the different coloured doves. The red dove is Christ; he rules over the others and gathers them into his dovecote. He also redeems through his blood as a result of his Passion. Black signifies the Law, which is obscure and needs interpretation, the speckled signifies the diversity of the twelve prophets. Sky-blue signifies Elijah, ascending to heaven in a chariot; the ashen brings to mind Jonah in his sackcloth, wearing ashes for penance. Gold

Eugen von Blaas, *Feeding the Pigeons*, 1877.

signifies the three young men who dared to challenge King Nebuchadnezzar (Daniel 3:18). Elisha is assigned the colour of honey. White represents John the Baptist and his baptism; silver is for Stephen, the first martyr.[62]

In Islam doves are held to be sacred. This is unusual in that neither pigeons nor doves are mentioned in the Koran, yet

A minaret in Iraq inhabited by pigeons.

reverence is shown to them by Muslims. About 1915 there was a pigeon shrine known as Kaptar-Mazzar near Hotan in Xinjiang, where Muslims would dismount and approach the area with reverence. In Istanbul there is a Mosque of Doves. Around the holy building the nests are kept safe, for they are not allowed to be disturbed. Special niches are left in the walls to allow them to roost there. It is said that a dove whispered in Mohammed's ear. This was an act of deception; he had concealed several seeds in his ear. When the dove was seen to be whispering in his ear, Mohammed convinced the onlookers that he was receiving Allah's sacred commands, via the dove. Shakespeare gave a mention of this to the Dauphin: 'Was Mahomet inspired with a dove?' (1 Henry VI 1:2) This action of the dove was not confined to Islam: at the Vatican, a servant was surprised to see Pope Gregory the Great's dove, which was always on his shoulder, 'dictating'.

The dove had a significant role to play in the founding of the capital of Egypt by the Muslim 'Amr ibn al-'As. When 'Amr invaded Egypt he and his army were there for several years, and 'Amr was becoming frustrated that the conquest hadn't been completed. He ordered his army to advance northwards to Alexandria. As they were preparing to leave, they noticed that a dove had made her nest on top of 'Amr's tent and had laid her eggs in it. 'Let her be,' said 'Amr, 'for she has taken refuge under our protection. The tent shall remain here until her chicks are hatched and she herself has flown away.'[63] A guard was posted to ensure that the dove was unharmed. In time a settlement was established on the site, and became known as al-Fustat ('the town of the tent'). These were the beginnings of modern-day Cairo.

In Hinduism the pigeon is a messenger of the god of death and justice, Yama.[64] Yama's master, Shiva, had become annoyed

Jean-Léon Gérôme, *Harem Women Feeding Pigeons in a Courtyard*, 1894, oil on canvas.

with certain human followers. In the end Shiva turned them into pigeons, which still haunt Shiva's temples and shrines, hoping to be released and changed back into their former human form. Some target the pigeon as an ominous bird in Hindu cultures, perhaps because of its association with death. There are charms to recite to ward off ill: 'Oh ye gods, if the pigeon has been sent as the messenger of Nirriti [cited as a destructive god] and has come to find us, we are prepared to sing his praises and we shall prepare a ransom.'[65] The pigeon is linked with death because it has come to symbolize reincarnation. Thousands of pigeons are fed daily in Hindu temples. In *Gay-Neck: The Story of a Pigeon*, the importance of the pigeon in Hinduism is emphasized at the beginning:

> Every third Hindu boy has perhaps a dozen pet carriers, tumblers, fantails, and pouters. The art of domesticating pigeons goes back thousands of years in India, and she has contributed two species of pigeons as a special product of her bird fanciers, the fantail and the pouter. Love and care have been showered on pigeons for centuries by emperors, princes, and queens in their marble palaces, as well as by the poor in their humble homes. The gardens, grottoes, and fountains of the Indian rich, the small field of flowers and fruits of the common folks, each has its ornament and music – many-coloured pigeons and cooing white doves with ruby eyes.[66]

Sikhs feed pigeons to honour the high priest and warrior Guru Govind Singh, who was a known friend of the pigeon. Sikhs also feed pigeons because they believe that when they are reincarnated they will never know hunger if they have fed pigeons in their previous life.

A girl and her attendants watching pigeons (according to register, on a verandah). India, opaque colour on paper, c. 1840.

In Gujarat in India, beautiful dovecotes are built known as Chabutras (from the Gujarati for 'pigeon').[67] They are raised platforms which are covered by a dome or roof. Plants and flowers adorn the structure. These birds are believed to embody the souls of the departed, and are held in great reverence. In 1921 in Bombay (Mumbai), two European boys killed a couple of doves in the street. The horror this caused closed down the stock exchange and there was a near riot.

Among the Native Americans, the dove also represents the cycle of reincarnation. The Pueblo Indians regarded the dove as an honoured bird. Its feathers were worn and also used to decorate prayer sticks (though this use depended on the tribe). The dove was viewed as a life-saver, for its song was thought to indicate where water could be found. Its feathers were worn on masks during rain-making rituals. The cries of the doves were said to be a call for rain; hence some of the Pueblo rain chants imitated the calls of doves. One song, sung as corn is being ground, goes:

Dove, you liar,
You are always telling the corn maidens
That there is water over here and over there.[68]

There is a Cherokee legend about a great famine when a pigeon was sent to see if she could find anything to eat (echoing the Flood narrative).[69] She returned with news of a country rich in crops, so the animals moved there.

Some Native Americans thought that the dove contained the soul of a lover. Anyone who hurt or killed a dove would be cursed.

In the social organization of the Blackfoot Indians of Montana, the hierarchy of the All Comrades Society had as its first two ranks Little Birds, which consisted of boys between the ages of fifteen and twenty, and Pigeons, men who had gone to war several times.[70]

In Asia the dove plays an important role. In China the dove represents longevity, faithfulness and spring. In Japan doves were sacred to Hachiman, God of War. Here we perceive another paradox: they were sacred to the God of War, yet if they were portrayed with a sword, then they indicated peace, for this signified the end of war. If we examine the tale of a mythical hero,

Eye decoration above the dome of the Great Stupa of Boudhanath, Kathmandu (Nepal).

Yorimoto, we understand this paradox better. When Yorimoto was being pursued by his enemies, he sought shelter in the hollow of a tree. A pair of doves flew out as the enemy passed by, so they assumed that there was no one in the tree. Yorimoto became Shogun. He said that the birds had saved him, and were therefore able to bring good luck.[71]

Even in the art of alchemy, the dove/pigeon was important, for it was perceived as symbolizing sublimation. Sometimes dove feathers were viewed as an instrument of Diana. Pigeon dung was valuable, for Paracelsus claimed 'that if you buried gold in pigeon's dung, it increased'.[72] In the alchemical opus, 'Birds tend to be more prominent than beasts, since the rising of spirits or vapours under heat is so often symbolized by flight of birds.'[73]

Doves play a role in folklore as well. There is a superstition that if a dove flies into a sickroom, or bumps into the window, or circles the house, then death will come to the household. Another superstition concerned the use of pigeon feathers as

Colour woodblock print from the series *Sanjuroku I kurabe* (The Thirty-six Beauties Compared), Japanese, 19th century.

bedding material. Apparently this was considered unlucky for the person using the bed, who was thought to die a painful death.

In Richard Gough's *History of Myddle* (1701–2), he records an omen which accompanied the owners of Cayhowell Farm in Shropshire. The omen was that a pair of pigeons would visit the farm and remain there for between seven and fourteen days before the person's death, but then would leave immediately afterwards. Gough had observed this himself three times, and thought it was the same pair of pigeons each time. Interestingly, when the farm was let to a tenant, the pigeons appeared before he died. On a more optimistic note, if someone at the farm was sick, and the pigeons did not appear, then that meant that the person would recover.[74]

A commonly held superstition is that if a dove is seen near a mineshaft, there will be an accident in the mine. This appears to run contrary to their symbolism of love and peace, but picks up on the doves' association with death. The appearance of a dove hovering near the mouth of a coal pit in 1902 was enough to cause 300 men to refuse to go to work there:

> The men have been whispering their fears to each other for some time past, but the drastic action on Monday was probably the outcome of so-called evil omens which are said to have been heard in the mine . . . there is, of course, the usual tale of the dove hovering over the mouth of the level.[75]

There were rumours of a dove being spotted in the area prior to the Llanbradach, Morfa Colliery and Senghenydd explosions.

Certain birds were associated with changing weather patterns; the pigeon heralded the promise of better weather soon to arrive.[76] In Surtees's *History . . . of Durham* (1816–40), he writes of the village of Stobb Cross:

> And here Stobcross 'brings on a village tale.' A few fields to the South stands a ruined dove-cote, shaded by a few straggling ashes, and haunted by a brood of wood-pigeons. Here a poor girl put herself down for love, in the homely phrase of the country, on the very spot of her appointments with her traitor lover; and her spirit still hovers round the cote, the scene of her earthly loves and

sorrows, in the form of a milk-white dove, distinguished
from its companions by three distinct crimson spots on
the breast.[77]

Surtees was told by an old farmer that he had seen this dove
twenty times, and, when seen, it heralded good weather and a
bountiful harvest.[78]

Doves and pigeons symbolize love, particularly when there
are two birds together:

Go dig my grave wide and deep
Place a marble slab at my head and feet

And over my coffin, place a snow white dove
To warn the world that I died of love.[79]

In parts of Europe doves were seen as a way to discover whom a young girl was to marry. If she took nine steps forwards and then nine steps backwards when she heard the first dove of spring coo, a hair of the intended would be found in her shoe.[80] Doves and pigeons were also attributed with the granting of one's heart's desire; if you made a wish after having seen the first dove of that year, then your wish would come true.

The pigeon has had a significant role in religion, ritual and culture for centuries: from providing the physical means for sacrifice, to becoming a religious symbol, the pigeon has played its part in creation myths, legends and folklore. Many cultures, including Western society, still associate the dove with the feminine, either as a symbol of motherhood or as a representation of the innocent or pure. It does seem strange that for such an important bird, these contributions are often associated with the 'dove' but not with the 'pigeon'. While there may be disagreement and no likelihood of assent regarding some of the practices or beliefs listed in this chapter, many would agree that the dove has become a universal symbol of peace, having played this role centuries before as a means of sacrifice to appease the gods, and/or by its willingness to find dry land for an ark whose inhabitants were searching for a new beginning.

An Uneasy Relationship:
Medicine, Meat and Messengers

MEDICINE

Pigeons were believed to possess healing properties. Their use for medicinal purposes ranged from common sense (i.e. as a source of good nutrition) to something smacking of folklore and superstition. In Roman times, Pliny the Elder wrote that ingesting pigeon blood was a means of curing bloodshot eyes.[1] During the seventeenth century eating pigeon flesh was seen as a form of protection against the plague and similar diseases: 'Those who make it their constant and ordinary food are seldom seized by the pestilential diseases.'[2] Squabs were the food of choice for invalids and others who were frail or convalescing. They were small, highly nutritious and easy to digest. In the eighteenth century the merits of squabs were recommended highly: 'They are nourishing, somewhat binding, strengthening and provoke urine: they are looked upon to be good for cleaning the Reins [kidneys] and to expel the Gross Matters that stick there.'[3]

Live pigeons were cut in half, and applied to the head or to the soles of the feet, because 'clapt hot upon the head mitigates fierce humours and discusses [i.e. dispels] melancholy sadness.'[4] Similar treatment was administered to Catherine of Braganza, the queen of Charles II. Samuel Pepys, in a diary entry of 19 October 1663, wrote: 'It seems she was so ill as to be shaved and pigeons put to her feet.'[5] When John Donne was seriously ill, he received the same treatment, in order to 'draw the vapours from the head'.[6] Pigeon dung was dried and sifted in order to make poultices and was reported to cure baldness and gout, as well as being ingested as medicine, or used to make an enema. The birds were also thought to prevent death due to snake bite. The pigeon's anus was placed on the wound; perhaps the lime neutralized the venom.[7] Passenger pigeons were slaughtered and their gizzards, entrails, blood and dung marketed as

The use of carrier pigeons to help break the Siege of Paris, 1870–71.

89

medical cures for a variety of conditions, including gallstones, dysentery, epilepsy, colic and fever.

If pigeons were truly regarded as vermin, would people risk their health by using them in order to be cured? Are humans prepared to put aside prejudice in the off chance of a cure? Would we do so today? Although 'pigeon' may not be an ingredient on pharmacists' shelves in the West, cannabis may have come to us via the pigeon. Pigeons had been observed ingesting cannabis seeds, and their reactions noted. Perhaps their intoxicated state led to the use of cannabis as a drug for humans.[8]

In recent times (though not as a pharmaceutical drug) pigeons have played a unique role in health care. The Department of Haematology at the Freedom Fields Hospital in Plymouth, Devon, utilized pigeons in order to save money as well as to ensure speedy delivery. In the late 1970s the Department, which serviced 20 hospitals in the area, realized that it was costing them approximately $40,000 per year to send blood samples in taxis and other means of transport from outlying areas to the central laboratory for testing. It was noted that there was a large number of racing homers in the area. The Department decided to trial racing homers with blood collections. The Devon Orthopaedic Association devised special carrier pouches made of soft chamois leather.[9] The first trial took place on 5 May 1977, with six pigeons flying from the general hospital at Green Bank, with blood samples in their pouches. The trip took seven minutes. This trial was proven to be a success, so a loft was set up adjacent to the Department of Haematology with a stock of young pigeons. It was estimated that during its first year of operation, there would be a saving of $42,000.[10]

This is not the only example of the use of homing pigeons for medical purposes. In rural Pennsylvania, a region where telephones were rare (because it was a predominantly Amish and Mennonite community), a local doctor built a loft and then left a homer at a number of farms. During the first year of operation, pigeons were boarding at 40 farms, and there was a waiting list of homes that wanted a bird as soon as they were bred and then trained. Messages were delivered to the doctor via the homer.[11]

In recent times, a homing pigeon has been linked with drugs of an illegal nature. Bosnian police have jailed a pigeon after discovering that prisoners had been using the bird in order to smuggle drugs into one of the country's highest security jails. It is suspected that heroin had been contained within tiny bags that had been strapped to the pigeon's legs.[12]

MEAT

Pigeons have been a food source for centuries. They have been trapped in flight, shot or bred and raised in dovecotes. Their domestication meant there would be a ready supply of meat for household consumption and for sacrifice.

On several Egyptian wall paintings and decorative reliefs there are pictures of pigeons being offered as food to the deceased. Pigeon bones have been found in the remains of a funerary meal in an excavated tomb from 3000 BC.[13] In antiquity young pigeons were a preferred food source for many. During Roman times writings by Cato the Elder, Pliny and Juvenal describe raising pigeons for the table in some detail.[14] Taxes on dovecotes were levied by Augustus. The Roman gourmet Apicius included pigeon as one of the ingredients in his cookery books, written in the first century AD, accompanied by sauce recipes to serve with roasted or boiled pigeon squabs.

Raising pigeons for the table (or for their dung, as was the case for Muslims) required housing. Dovecotes, often constructions

Pigeon Shooting, 1832, hand-coloured etching, aquatint paper. London, published by Robert Pollard.

of great architectural beauty, were built. They may be aesthetically pleasing, with romantic associations (the cooing of doves turning one's thoughts to love and settling down with a mate), but the reality is they were solely for storing flock, in the manner of a barn for larger animals. In the Middle East the first dovecotes were fashioned from clay pots, which were stuck together and placed in the areas where the pigeons would gather. In other areas of the Mediterranean clay pots were often hung upon the outside walls of dwellings.

In the classical world, Roman writers borrowed the Greek terms *peristerion* and *peristerotrophion* (dovecote) and added a new term, *columbarium*, to describe a dovecote.[15] In *De rerum rusticarum*, Varro wrote about the type of dwelling:

> The *peristerion* is built in the shape of a large *testudo* with a vaulted roof. It has a narrow entrance and windows latticed in the Carthaginian fashion, or wider than these are, and finished in a double lattice so that the whole

place may be well lit and no snake or other noxious animal may be able to get in.[16]

Varro goes on to mention that dovecotes were to be found in Rome, Florence and in the countryside. Pigeons were also kept in turrets, or housed in the gable ends of houses.

In some areas of Iran dovecotes from the seventeenth century have survived, elegant and large in scale, as they were built by the ruler of the time. Some are over 21 metres (70 feet) tall, and would have housed more than 10,000 pigeons.[17]

The eighteenth-century naturalist George-Louis Leclerc, Comte de Buffon, wrote of the dovecote and its inhabitants:

To induce the Pigeons to settle we must erect a lofty building, well-covered without and fitted up with numerous cells. They really are not domestics like dogs and horses; or prisoners like fowls: they are rather voluntary captives, transient guests who continue to reside in the dwellings assigned them only because they like it and are pleased with the situation which affords abundance of food, and all the conveniences and comforts of life.[18]

In parts of Europe having a dovecote and raising pigeons for one's table became an indicator of class. Pigeon had long been a culinary delicacy in England for the landed gentry. Laws were passed forbidding anyone but the nobility permission to raise pigeons. In England pigeons were fed little during feudal times. Instead the birds were encouraged to feed on the crops of their feudal tenants. The law forbade tenants to complain:

Some men may make it a Case of Conscience, whether a Man may have a Pigeon House, because his Pigeons eat other Folk's Corn. But there is no such thing as Conscience in the Business: the Matter is, whether he is a Man of Such Quality that the State allows him to have a Dove House: if so, there is an end of the Business: his Pigeons have a right to eat where they please themselves.[19]

It has been estimated that a thousand pairs of pigeons can consume 200 tons of grain per year.[20] If we consider the outrage at the loss of grain, plus the fact that tenants had no legal redress, then it is understandable that tempers would be high and the channels of bitterness running deep. In early medieval times, dovecotes were sometimes built on common land or wasteland to lessen the damage to cultivated land. The reverse was the case in France and Scotland, 'where the law decreed that accommodation had to be built well within the owner's land in an attempt to confine the birds' damage to his own crops.'[21]

In France, too, dovecotes, or pigeonniers, were only for the nobility. The French Revolution, however, changed the course of dovecote ownership forever. The dovecote's link with nobility led to a severing of ties on 14 July 1789. The wording in the draft of the Declaration of Rights stated that pigeonniers were to be abolished. Later, it was suggested that the existing pigeonniers be destroyed as well; however, due to a last minute intervention, this was amended on 6 August. The amendment read:

> The exclusive right to have a fuie or a dovecote is hereby abolished; the pigeons will be kept enclosed within the dovecotes at times set by local communities, and, during these periods any pigeons flying about will be regarded as fair game: everyone will have the right to kill them.[22]

Other countries had tough laws as well. In Scotland, parents were to be fined 13 shillings and four pence if their children entered a dovecote, and the children were to be whipped. Anyone found shooting at a pigeon faced a prison sentence of forty days.[23] When James VI of Scotland ascended the English throne, severe laws were brought into the English realm. During the first year of his reign, a new law was enacted which stated that anyone who killed a pigeon would face three months in prison 'unless a twenty shilling fine for each bird was paid to the Churchwarden of the offender's parish'.[24]

Preceding the development of hardy winter crops, which would allow cattle to be kept all year round, pigeons, producing two squabs eight to ten times a year for up to seven years, meant a regular and dependable source of food. Pigeon husbandry was low maintenance; due to inborn homing instincts, they would return to the nest each evening. In a rhyming calendar for husbandry, January was set aside for the care of the doves:

> Feed Doves but kill not
> If loose them ye will not
> Dove house repair
> Make douve hole fair
> For hop ground cold
> Douve doung worth gold.[25]

They lived harmoniously in a confined area, within an established community. A well-fed flock would tend to stay put. Cruel practices were few, one exception being the Roman practice of force-feeding squabs. Sometimes the fattening-up period was hastened by breaking their legs to confine them to the nest.[26]

In Europe different types of pigeon were raised and bred for the purposes of eating. In Spain and Italy it was the Runt, which was the largest of the domestic pigeons. The French craved a still larger bird, so the Mondaine was bred, which became a favourite of the Dutch and Flemish.

In England 'spatchcocked' pigeon is an old recipe. Young birds were culled at the age of four weeks. They were 'despatched' (*spatch*) quickly and then 'cooked' (*cocked*) when the cockbirds were culled from the dovecote.[27]

Dovecotes were not listed in the Domesday Book (1086), so it is suggested that the Normans introduced domestication of the pigeon to England. They certainly brought with them the feudal right to own a dovecote. Many of the medieval churches had dovecotes, or 'pigeon holes', within their walls, and these were viewed as church property. They were owned by abbeys

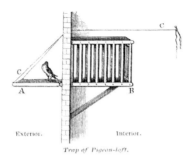

Trap of pigeon loft
from E. S. Dixon,
*The Dovecote
and the Aviary*
(London, 1851).

Trap of Pigeon-loft.

A, the door of the trap (outside the building).
B, the inner end of the trap where the swinging doors hang.
C C, the string used to pull up the outer door of the trap.

Trap of Pigeon-loft.
Interior showing the loose bars called "the bolt.
B, the little swinging doors on the inner end.
C, the string which pulls up the outer door.

and priories, and were a valuable asset. Many monasteries had large dovecotes to supply meat to the community; some orders would abstain from consuming four-legged animals, but would allow fowls and pigeons to be eaten.

As the use of pigeons became popular, dovecotes increased across Europe, with the exception of the Scandinavian countries and Switzerland. Perhaps this was due to a lack of large areas of arable land.[28] A wide variety of designs of dovecotes can be found in different countries, even within regions of the same country. In India, bottle-necked wells for pigeons were sunk underground and lined. Perhaps they were kept underground to protect the birds from the sun. This method is still used in parts of the Middle East and in Algeria.

The architecture of dovecotes reflects changes in building styles and advancements in animal husbandry. Even some of the older styles, such as the circular dovecote, had improvements made to their interiors, such as the invention of the potence, a ladder device which enabled eggs and squabs to be collected from all levels of the curved exterior dovecote. The curved wall was to deter cats, rats and other animals from being able to get into the building.

Superstitions abound in reference to protecting the pigeons from invaders, such as rats, cats, weasels, squirrels, ferrets, owls and other birds. Alongside conventional methods, such as tethering dogs outside the dovecotes, or encircling the building with prickly gorse and briars, sometimes charms were placed within the building. One, to deter weasels, was to hang upside down a rope with which a man had been hanged, or a wolf or stag's head.[29] Another practice widespread throughout Egypt, described by Pliny and still advocated in sixteenth-century England, was the burying of live or mummified kestrels in earthenware jars.[30] These jars were then buried beneath the dovecote or hung on its inner walls. It has been suggested that this practice stems from ancient Egypt, where falcons were sacrificed to the falcon-god Horus.[31] Perhaps these jars were placed in the dovecotes as a plea for protection, and to act as a charm to deter hawks.

Settling new territories created the opportunity to bring animals, including pigeons, to the new frontier. Christopher Columbus (whose surname is Latin for 'dove', *columba*) had a role in the introduction of domesticated pigeons as a food source. When Columbus returned to the Caribbean in 1493, he and 1,500 colonists took with them farm birds as well as caged rock doves.[32] Early colonists brought pigeons with them to the USA, along with other domestic animals and fowl. In 1795 General Greene wrote that his Mulberry Plantation (situated near Savannah, Georgia) had a pigeon house that accommodated a thousand birds.[33] Commercial squab production developed rather late as an industry in the United States, due to the abundance of wild game. It wasn't until the nineteenth century that it became a commercial enterprise. In 1901 Elmer C. Rice published his *Manual on the Breeding of Squabs by the Robinson Method.* In 1902 Johnson's Pigeon Ranch (situated outside Los Angeles) contained thousands of birds. By 1907 there were hundreds of commercial lofts throughout the USA.[34] The breeds used in the early days included Homers, Antwerps, Dragoons and the Duchess. Later, diners were requesting larger squabs, so the

A dovecote in rural America.

White King, the Giant Homer and the Mondaine were developed, as well as the importation of larger types, including the Carneau from France and Belgium.

BY-PRODUCTS

The most obvious by-product of the pigeon is pigeon down and feathers, which were used for pillows and quilts. Another was its dung. Although this was used as an ingredient in medicine, it appears to have been of more value as fertilizer. Throughout history, dung was a rich commodity. It was recorded that as a result of the famine during the siege of Samaria 'one-fourth of a kab of dove's dung [was sold] for five shekels of silver' (2 Kings 6:25). A kab equalled 2 quarts, so this dung was of great value. In Egypt pigeon dung has been collected for centuries as a mode of fertilizer, especially for the growing of melons. Dovecotes were built primarily for this purpose. Large palm leaf mats were placed across the beams below the columbarium; the pigeon droppings were collected and then sold in the local markets.

In 1651 Samuel Hartlib, a friend of John Milton, made the claim that one load of pigeon dung was 'worth 10 loads of other *dung* and therefore [was] usually sown on *wheate* that lieth a far off, and not easy to be helped.'[35] He added that it was excellent on hop gardens as well.

John Moore sang its praises, attributing its 'hot Nature' to the 'nitrous Quality wherewith it is endured'.[36] He went on to call it 'a very excellent Soil for a cold, moist natural Ground'. It would be sown along with the grain and harrowed in with it.

In France, Italy and Spain, pigeon dung was highly prized as fertilizer for the vineyards and hemp crops. Dung was also used for a time by tanners who were making soft leather. Apparently the dung helped in the process of hair removal from the skins.

At the end of the sixteenth century in England another use was found for pigeon dung as an important source of saltpetre, which was used in the manufacture of gun powder. In 1627 Charles I authorized the collection of pigeon dung from stables, farmyards and domestic households.[37] This collection was to take place for only two hours each day, and if any birds or eggs were lost in the process, the owner was entitled to compensation. This industry did not last long; by the end of the eighteenth century a natural source of saltpetre was discovered in South America and in the East Indies.[38]

Each pigeon defecates more than 10 kilograms of waste each year; perhaps, instead of complaining, city residents could put pigeon droppings to good use.

Pigeon blood has been used in fashionable red glass known as gorge-de-pigeon. This technique was common in European wine goblets in the early twentieth century. Pigeon blood is also a term used to describe the finest hue of ruby. Catherine the Great owned a ruby of true pigeon-blood red, the size of a pigeon's egg. In Burmese, the word 'ko-twe' means 'pigeon's blood'. It is used in the ancient Burmese system of classification of rubies. The grading 'ko-twe' is given to the highest quality of ruby, the one with the finest hue.[39] True pigeon-blood rubies come from Mogok, in Upper Burma. Some have compared the colour of the ruby to the centre of a live pigeon's eye, or to the colour of the first two drops of blood from the nose of a freshly killed Burmese pigeon. 'It must be stressed that the true pigeon's-blood red is extremely rare, more a colour of the mind than the material world. One Burmese trader expressed it best when he said "asking to see the pigeon's blood is like asking to see the face of God."'[40]

The use of the term 'pigeon-blood' to describe the hue of rubies has annoyed some. In 1985 James Nelson, who discouraged the use of fanciful terms or phrases, decided to settle this matter:

In an attempt to seek a more quantitative description for this mysterious red colour known only to hunters and the few fortunate owners of the best Burmese rubies, the author sought the help of the London Zoo. Their Research Department were quick to oblige and sent a specimen of fresh, lysed, aerated, pigeon's blood. A sample was promptly spectrophotometered . . .The Burmese bird can at last be safely removed from the realms of gemmology and consigned back to ornithology.[41]

It is important to put aside the more common Western use of 'pigeon' as a degrading term. As noted in chapter Two, at different times in history pigeons have been held in high regard; to have a ruby named after pigeon blood would have been viewed as a compliment, rather than as a slight. According to Diane Morgan, pre-Buddhist Burma observed a form of animism.[42] One of the practices to appease the spirits was to kill chickens or pigeons.

MESSENGERS AND MEDALS

Pigeons have helped change and chart the course of history as a means of communication. They have carried messages since before the time of Hannibal, who used pigeon post while crossing the Alps. Pigeons carried information for King Solomon (950 BC), and a large-scale network was set up by Cyrus the Great in the sixth century BC, covering the Achaemenid Persian empire.[43] Alexander the Great used pigeons to relay information, as did Julius Caesar during his campaign to take over Gaul. Pliny records that Hirtius and Decimus Iunius Brutus communicated via pigeons at the siege of Mutina (Modena) in 43 BC. Frontinus wrote:

Hirtius also shut up pigeons in the dark, starved them, fastened letters to their necks by a hair, and then released them as near to the city walls as he could. The birds, eager for light and food, sought the highest buildings and were received by Brutus, who in that way was informed of everything, especially after he set food in certain spots and taught the pigeons to alight there.[44]

As well as conveying news from the battlefields, pigeons were used by the Romans to announce victories at the amphitheatre. In Greece, the message-bearing pigeons were linked with the Oracles, as well as with the early Olympic Games. According to Ovid, Taurosthenes stained a pigeon bright purple and released it, announcing his victory at the Olympic Games to his son in Aegina. This set a trend, and served to alert others to the identity of the winners.

China has had a long tradition of pigeon post, dating from the beginning of the fifth century. News ranged from the important, such as news from bankers and businessmen, to the more mundane, such as the issuing of dinner invitations.[45] Pigeon whistles, made out of bamboo pipes, were attached to the leg or rump feathers. Music was heard when the pigeons were in flight. Some thought of the sound as being the voices of their ancestors' spirits. The sound may have helped ward off predators as well.

During the Crusades, homing pigeons were an essential item of most knights' luggage.[46] At certain intervals along the route, they were released to relay news to those at home. In the middle of May 1099, the Crusaders had finally reached their destination, the Holy City of Jerusalem. Thomas Fuller, in his *Historie of the Holy Warre* (1643), wrote:

When the first light brought news of morning, they [fought] on afresh because they had intercepted a letter tied to the legs of a dove, it being the fashion of that country both to write and send their letters with the wings of a fowl, wherein the Persian Emperor promised present succour to the besieged.[47]

The news encouraged the Christians to continue, which they did, the Holy City becoming under their control.

Pigeon post relayed other news of battles during the Crusades, such as the fall of Constantinople in 1204. A pigeon was sent back to Venice, a flight of over 700 miles, with the good news.[48] The use of pigeons was advantageous for the other side as well. The landing of the crusading party led by Louis IX of France in 1249 was reported by homing pigeons to the Sultan of Cairo. This allowed them to change tactics and surprise the invaders.

The establishment of pigeon outposts became common throughout the Middle East, a valued means of communication between the larger cities. The first recorded pigeon post is listed as 1150 in Baghdad. This post was in constant use until 1258, when raiding bands from Mongolia ate all of the pigeons.[49] This incident, however, did not deter the setting up of other pigeon posts across the Middle East and within Europe. Most of the trained pigeons were brought to Europe by the Crusaders, and later, in the sixteenth century, from Persia. Some of these networks were quite complex; in the fourteenth century in Turkey, pigeon towers were built, spaced at about 40 miles apart. Messages were carried from one bird and transferred to the next, similar to a relay race, with a duplicate message sent two hours later to ensure that the message got through.[50]

The ancient maritime civilizations, particularly Phoenician and Egyptian sailors, used pigeons to aid commerce, for they would release the birds to announce the arrival of their sailing ships as well as to carry other messages. Fishermen continued this practice; they would release a pigeon to announce their catch, or something similar, before their arrival. In the USA during Prohibition (1919–33) pigeon post was used by bootleggers as a means of communication between ships and land bases. For many years, ocean liners carried homers as part of their cargo, as a form of insurance in case radio signals failed.

By the nineteenth century pigeon post was firmly established throughout many parts of Europe. At 30–70 miles per hour pigeons were faster than mail coaches or horseback, and they were used to fill in gaps in the transport system, particularly between Paris and Berlin. Their ability to 'home', as well as their speed, was capitalized on. Until the invention of the telegraph (1836) and the telephone (1875), pigeons were still the fastest way to convey messages. Stock market reports were sent via homing pigeons. In 1815 the Rothschild Bank in London was able to take advantage of the news of Napoleon's defeat at

Messenger pigeons on a 15th-century woodcut from an edition of Sir John Mandeville's *Travels*.

Pigeon Post,
German woodcut,
1488.

Waterloo.[51] In England pigeons were used by football supporters
to convey the scores of games played away from home. *The Times*
newspaper set up a pigeon post between London and Boulogne,
whilst stockbrokers had their own lofts at Dover and Folk-
stone.[52] By the end of the nineteenth century other newspapers
used pigeon post to record events at home, for other sporting
news, such as the results of the Derby and boat races. In 1845
Reuters news agency started its European business by using
homing pigeons, initially with 45 pigeons, and having them
travel between Aachen in Germany and Brussels. For many years
concrete lofts were built on the rooftops of newspaper companies in Japan. In 1959 when the city of Nagoya was isolated and
wrecked by a typhoon, pigeons brought back pictures of the
devastation to newspaper editors elsewhere.[53]

Pigeon post was also used to decrease the sense of isolation.
On remote banana, tea and coffee plantations planters would

send their pigeons to nearby towns with a list of provisions needed. Some mining operations relied on pigeons to relay messages for them. On Great Barrier Island off the coast of New Zealand, pigeons were the messengers for the miners who wanted to communicate with people in Auckland. In Tasmania pigeons were supplied to the lighthouse keepers, but this proved to be a problem, for at the end of three months, some of the pigeons saw the lighthouse as their home and would not return to the mainland.[54]

The first organized pigeon airmail service began in 1896 between New Zealand and the Great Barrier Reef. The sinking of the ss *Wairarapa* off the Great Barrier Reef with the loss of 134 lives was the catalyst, for news of the disaster didn't reach New Zealand for three days. Special pigeon-gram stamps were issued costing 2' (20 cents) each, with the fee paid in cash before the pigeon was released. In the Northern Hemisphere, the first airmail stamp was carried by pigeons in 1898. The last remaining pigeon post was abandoned in India in 2004, with the birds being retired to live out the rest of their days in peace.

Pigeons could be employed as a means of saving money. In 1937 this case of deception made the press:

A commuting family possessed a single transportation pass, and the members of this family left for work at varying times. Each member of the family carried a pigeon to work. Upon reaching his destination, he released the bird with the pass which was then used by another member of the family leaving at a somewhat later hour. Either two or three flights a day for this purpose were made.[55]

Pigeons allowed communication to continue during war. In *The Black Tulip*, Alexandre Dumas *père* records something of the

Message cylinder
attached to a
carrier pigeon.

Australian postage
stamp celebrating
the International
Year of Peace,
1986.

War of Independence in Holland, particularly the 6-month siege of Leiden by the Spaniards in 1574, when the citizens were saved by pigeons delivering messages from the outside world.

In the course of the Siege of Paris (19 September 1870 to 28 January 1871) during the Franco-Prussian War, balloons carrying Parisian pigeons were released from Paris and flown to London, Tours and other cities. From there they were released with messages to be delivered back to the Parisians. This means of communication was arranged by the British General Post Office.[56] During the months of the siege, more than 150,000 official and 1,000,000 private messages were flown into Paris. It was during the Siege that better ways of delivering the messages were perfected. At first the messages were of paper, wrapped tightly and then waxed and attached to a tail feather. This method, however, was not successful, and as a result many messages were lost. The process was refined by inserting the message into a small goose quill and tying it with waxen thread to the strongest

tail feather.[57] Later, micro-photography was perfected, and films of collodion were carried by the pigeon. When the messages reached their destination, they were projected onto a screen with a magic lantern and the messages written down.[58] Pigeon post was so successful that the French authorities opened it to personal letters. The use of pigeons during the Siege of Paris was described in Arnold Bennett's *The Old Wives' Tale.*

The Prussians tried to intercept the pigeons by the use of hawks, but many of the pigeons reached their destination. This is even more remarkable when we consider that the siege took place during the winter months.

The success of the pigeon messengers led to the establishment of military pigeon stations in Europe, preparing them for future wars. It also meant a rise in popularity of the sport of pigeon

Jules Didier (1831–92) and Jacques Guiaud (1811–76), *Les pigeons messagers*, 1870, oil on canvas.

Japanese carrier pigeon troops.

racing. At the outbreak of World War I, British authorities banned the use of pigeons, for they feared espionage. Captain A. H. Osman convinced the British authorities of the skills of pigeons, and how they would assist when technology failed. The potential of pigeons to transmit messages was harnessed by minesweeping trawlers; and in the early stages of the war, before wireless had been fitted to U-boats, pigeons were the means by which an SOS message was conveyed, and the crew saved.[59] These examples led to the establishment of the British Pigeon Service. Unlike her European allies, where military lofts had been established, in Britain the use of pigeons was entirely voluntary. It was not until March 1916 that they were sent to the Front. Pigeons (homers) were dropped from planes in baskets, into friendly areas, in order to return with messages. British War Records show that 95 per cent of the pigeons got through with their messages.[60]

Killing, wounding or molesting a homing pigeon was an offence under the Defence of the Realm Act regulations. Pigeons were vital for carrying important messages. It must have been hard for poorly fed soldiers to resist this food source. If caught, offenders faced a heavy fine of £100 or six months' imprisonment.[61] Posters and notices concerning the protection of the pigeon were placed around the trenches.

By December 1915 over 200 pigeons had been mobilized as part of fifteen pigeon stations on the Western Front. Not all was smooth flying; on 18 October 1914, as German forces were advancing on Antwerp, 'the head of the Belgian Pigeon Service "with tears streaming down his face" . . . burned alive 2,500 of his potential messengers rather than let them fall into the hands of the Kaiser's advancing troops.'[62]

The Battle of the Somme demonstrated how useful and vital the pigeon service was. The French used 5,000 pigeons during the battle, with only 2 per cent of the pigeons failing to get through.[63] This did not mean that 2 per cent of the messages were undelivered; all essential messages were sent in duplicate by other birds. Mobile lofts, drawn by horse, or converted omnibuses, were introduced, and these could be moved quickly to different locations. Messages were sent from trenches to the battalion headquarters, and from tanks to their base. By the end of the war, 22,000 pigeons were in service with British forces, looked after by over 400 pigeoneers.[64]

As soon as Germany invaded Belgian or French territory, orders were issued demanding that all pigeons were to be destroyed. Anyone found either selling them, or holding on to them as their owner, was accused of possessing contraband of war, and thereby severely punished.

On the Western Front, a French pigeon was awarded both the Croix de Guerre and the Légion d'honneur; a memorial to the pigeon is situated at Verdun. A monument at Lille in France was erected to commemorate the 20,000 birds killed in action, and a war memorial in Brussels pays tribute to 21,000 pigeons and their fanciers who died in wartime. In Berlin there is a monument to German war pigeons.

Major General Fowler, Chief of the Department of Signals and Communications in the British Army, wrote:

> If it became necessary immediately to discard every line and method of communications used on the front, except one, and it were left to me to select that one method, I should unhesitatingly choose the pigeons. It is the pigeons on which we must and do depend when every other method fails. During the quiet periods we can rely on telephone, telegraph, flag signals, our dogs, and various other

During WWI pigeons were protected from becoming an easy source of food because they were needed for the war effort.

DEFENCE OF THE REALM
Regulation 21A.

SHOOTING HOMING PIGEONS.

Killing, Wounding or Molesting Homing Pigeons is punishable under the Defence of the Realm Regulations by

SIX MONTHS IMPRISONMENT OR £100 FINE.

The Public are reminded that Homing Pigeons are doing valuable work for the Government, and are requested to assist in the suppression of the shooting of these birds.

£5 REWARD

will be paid by the NATIONAL HOMING UNION for information leading to the conviction of any person SHOOTING HOMING PIGEONS the property of its Members.

Information should be given to the Police, Military Post, or to the Secretary of the Union, C. C. PLACKETT, 14, EAST PARADE, LEEDS.

ways in use on the front with the British armies. But when the battle wages and everything gives way to barrage and machine gun fire, to say nothing of gas attacks and bombing, it is TO THE PIGEON THAT WE GO FOR SUCCOUR ... I am glad to say they have never failed us.[65]

On the front lines in Europe mobile lofts were kept behind trenches. Often pigeons had to fly through gunfire and poisonous gas in order to deliver their messages to base. In England fixed lofts were established at key aerodromes. A line of lofts were built along the eastern coastline, from Newcastle upon Tyne to Hastings, so that they could be utilized in the event of an invasion. All crews of tanks, seaplanes and submarines, which carried pigeons, were instructed in how to handle and care for the pigeons in their care. There was a high casualty rate amongst the pigeons involved in the Intelligence Service; only 10 per cent of homing pigeons sent to sympathizers and members of the resistance managed to return.[66]

Belgian army pigeons.

A message is rolled up and placed into a container that is attached to the leg of a carrier pigeon. 61st Divisional Signals, Ballymena, Northern Ireland, 3 July 1943.

One of the most remarkable pigeons was named Cher Ami ('Dear Friend'), a blue chequered cock, who saved the members of the 'Lost Battalion' of New York's 77th Division of the US Army. On 27 October 1918 at Grand Pré, the soldiers were under heavy attack, and there was only one bird left to be released, the others having perished due to enemy gunfire. Cher Ami was released, and then was hit by enemy fire, but he managed to reach his loft at Rampont, a distance of 40 miles in 25 minutes, close to death. The message cylinder was still attached to his wounded leg, which was hanging together by a few strips of sinew. Thanks to his bravery, the battalion was quickly rescued. Cher Ami was awarded the French Croix de Guerre but no

American decoration, since the US military do not honour their animals in war service in this fashion, although he did receive a gold medal from American racing pigeon fancier organizations. Cher Ami died from his battle wounds on 13 June 1919. News about his feats became well known, the stuff of legend. In 1919 a film was made about his bravery, and in 1926 a poem was penned:

Mon Cher Ami – that's my dear friend
You are the one we'll have to send;
The whole battalion now is lost,
And you must win at any cost.[67]

During World War II, wild pigeons were not held in the same high regard as their homing ancestors. Instead, wild wood pigeons were seen as agricultural pests, and a useful addition to the food table during a time of food rationing. At the time, there were 5 or 6 million wood pigeons in Britain. Free cartridges were given to marksmen, which resulted in over one million wood pigeons supplementing the meat market during World War II.[68]

In June 1940 pigeon fanciers were being encouraged to volunteer their birds for service, getting information from occupied Europe. The pigeons would be taken to airfields, fitted with metal message containers, and then placed into a single bird box which had a parachute attached, as well as food supplies to last 10 days.[69] The boxes also contained instructions and questionnaires for the finders, who were to send the bird back with the information. The round trip could cover 300 miles. Some were felled by German-organized hawks posted across the Pas de Calais. In total, over a quarter of a million messenger pigeons were in active service during World War II. The heroics of the pigeon during wartime were brought to the public's attention in

A pigeon
parachute
from WWI.

the animated film *Valiant*. The film, about the pigeon corps delivering an important message from the underground back to HQ in England, was a combination of several incidents during World War II. The characters include a small but plucky wood pigeon, and a food-obsessed pigeon from Trafalgar Square (overweight and covered in fleas, conveying the disgust that many feel about the common rock pigeon). In order to deliver their messages, they have to dodge their true enemies, the hawks. In the film, these are fierce and crafty, portrayed as Nazis. In one scene, the main hawk threatens to eat one of the captured pigeons. The pigeon is outraged, saying that he thought he was vegetarian, a reference to Hitler's supposed vegetarianism.[70]

Two of the most famous breeders were Mussolini and Franklin Delano Roosevelt. Some of Roosevelt's pigeons carried messages to and from besieged Paris during World War II. Heinrich Himmler, head of the Gestapo, was a pigeon fancier and a former president of the German Pigeon Association. At the close of the war, an auction was held near Rome, the main draw for which was Mussolini's homing pigeons. Many pigeon fanciers travelled long distances in order to attend this event.

In the USA, at the peak of the war, the pigeon service consisted of 150 officers, 3,000 enlisted men and 54,000 pigeons. Approximately 30,000 messages were sent via pigeons while overseas during the war, with 96 per cent reaching their destination.

Some pigeons ended up as POWs. In the winter of 1944 the pigeon Lucia di Lammermoor was carried to a forward position. Released with important information, she was delayed in flight. That night she returned with a message: 'To the American Troops: Herewith we return a pigeon to you. We have enough to eat – The German Troops.'

When it was feared that Australia would be invaded, breeders from all areas of Australia donated pigeons, so that messages would get through if radio contact were impossible. When the war moved to New Guinea, pigeons had a vital role there as well. They were able to fly in mountainous areas and over the jungle, delivering messages in areas were military communication was difficult, or even impossible.

Pigeons were not conscripted, and no compensation was given for those that did not return. The reward for fanciers was knowing that their pigeons were making an important contribution to the war effort.[71] Having said this, those who did not make their pigeons available to the National Pigeon Service (in Britain) did not receive corn rations for their birds.

In 1943 Maria Dickin, the founder of the PDSA (People's Dispensary for Sick Animals), introduced the Dickin Medal, for heroic animals that were part of the war service. This award covered the Armed Forces and the Civil Defence units in World War II. The Dickin Medal, with its blue, brown and green ribbon, came to be viewed as the animal equivalent of the Victoria Cross for valour. On the bronze medal is inscribed 'For Gallantry', then 'We Also Serve'. During World War II the Dickin Medal was awarded to twenty-four dogs, three horses, one cat and thirty-two pigeons.[72] The first animal to receive the Dickin Medal was a blue-chequered pigeon named Winkie that saved the crew of a bomber. There were many who thought that the homing pigeon had had its day, since radio communication

The Dickin Medal, the animal equivalent of the Victoria Cross, was awarded to heroic animals for their war efforts. Pigeons received more Dickin Medals than any other animal.

was viewed as superior, but this did not take into account the times when radio messages could no longer be sent. This point can be illustrated by reference to the case of Winkie (so named because of the way her eyelid drooped with fatigue). In 1942 a British Beaufort was forced down into the North Sea. Winkie was thrown from her container and, against the odds, made worse by the oily water clogging her wing feathers, managed to fly 120 miles to the Scottish coast to get help. A rescue team located the crew, clinging to a dinghy, and they were brought to safety. It is heartening to note that several days later Winkie was the guest at a banquet held in her honour: 'She sat in her cage at the end of a long table and was toasted by admiring admirals.'[73]

In the PDSA Animal Cemetery in Ilford, Essex, there is a headstone to 'Mary of Exeter'. Mary the pigeon was enlisted in the Exeter Group on the National Pigeon Service lines of defensive communication. Her route was from Taunton to Exeter, as well as from Plymouth to Exeter. This pigeon flew many missions and had many wounds. On one occasion, she was released with a message from the US 8th Corps but went missing. Four days later, she dropped down on her loft, covered in blood. She had been ripped open from neck to breast, having been attacked by a falcon. She was stitched up and went back into service. She was wounded on two more occasions. At one time there were 22 stitches in her body, which weighed just one pound.

In Australia two pigeons were awarded the Dickin Medal. These two pigeons (Pigeon 139 DD 43 T and Pigeon 879 DD 43 Q) were the only Australian animal heroes to receive it. They were posthumous awards, for neither came home alive after the war. Keith Wrightson, a lieutenant with the Australian Corps of Signals' Pigeon Service in New Guinea during World War II, estimates that up to 10,000 were left behind in New Guinea.[74] Quarantine regulations, combined with the realization that

Frédéric Henri
Kay Henrion's
Dove of Peace
poster, c. 1944.

there were no natural grains suitable for them in New Guinea, meant that the pigeons were euthanized on humane grounds. Only a small number of pigeons were returned for display purposes. On 8 November 1945 this tribute was printed in the Sydney *Sun* newspaper, in memory of the nine New Guinea pigeons mounted for the Australian War Memorial exhibit:

> Now fare you well my faithful bird,
> In war you were a wizard.
> So now your country honours you
> By taking out your gizzard.[75]

Many of the soldiers were devastated that their fellow 'soldiers' were to be destroyed. They had trained them for war service, they had saved lives, bonds had been formed, and then their feathered comrades were to be killed rather than 'retired', as happened in other countries. Perhaps it is telling that the

Australian pigeons were given numbers, not names; a way to distance the formation of a bond?[76] In November 2000 an invitation was issued to former members of the Pigeon Section to attend the Remembrance Day ceremony at the Cenotaph in London's Whitehall; recognition at last.

Although Frédéric Henri Kay Henrion's 'Dove of Peace' of 1944 connects the dove with peace, it was Picasso's design of the dove on a poster for the World Peace Congress in 1949 which linked it in the psyche as a modern symbol of peace. The United Nations' dove is easily recognizable. Yet the dove as a universal symbol of peace has been challenged. Banksy's *Bethlehem*, a piece of provocative graffiti, challenges the dove and its associated message of peace. The use of the pigeon as a messenger during wartime could do the same.

Banksy's *Bethlehem* heralds a different Christmas message. Bethlehem series, December 2007.

In recent years pigeons have become smog monitors. In 2006 there was a plan to fit mobile backpacks to a flock of pigeons to monitor air pollution. Twenty pigeons would be released into the skies over San Jose, California, each carrying a GPS satellite tracking receiver, air pollution sensors and a basic mobile phone. Miniature cameras around their necks would also post aerial pictures. They would be messengers for the environment, continuing the role of their legendary ancestor, back in the time of the Flood. In that story, they were locating land; now they would be helping to preserve that heritage.

SPORT

The fantastic navigational skill of the pigeon has led to the sport of pigeon racing, similar to horse racing (and sometimes likened to 'racing for the "blue collar"'). The average speed of homing pigeons is 60 miles per hour, with spurts of 80–90 miles per hour. Modern racing started in Belgium, the earliest race being held in 1815. In 1819 there was a race from London to Antwerp, involving 32 birds. In 1832 there was another long-distance race between London and Belgium. Belgian pigeon fanciers developed pigeons specially cultivated for fast flight and long endurance called Voyageurs. The use of these pigeons spread to many parts of the world. By the 1880s other countries in Europe had racing clubs. In England, in the early days of pigeon racing, pigeons were either taken by boat to Southampton, or in horse-drawn coaches or in guards' vans of trains. At Marylebone Station, London, there was a 'Columbadrome' where the racing pigeons could relax before being taken to their destination.[77] Nowadays pigeons are taken to club rooms, crated and transported to the race point. It is a national sport in Belgium, with over 60,000 pigeon fanciers in a population of

10 million. It is also popular in other parts of Europe (there are more than 500 clubs in the Netherlands), as well as having a devoted following in the USA, where there are over 10,000 followers. Pigeon racing was introduced into the USA in 1875, and there has been regular racing since 1878. According to a recent survey by the American Racing Pigeon Union, there are 15,000 lofts registered in the USA. Some have seen this as a cruel sport and have campaigned to have it banned, successfully so in Chicago.

It is fast becoming a top sport in areas of Asia, as well as in Romania and Turkey, due to the high prize money available and the betting aspect of the sport. One of the highest sums ever paid for a pigeon was the £110,000 offered for Invincible Spirit after he won the Barcelona International classic race in 1992. There has been a downturn in recent years due to the cost of living, and the age of the fanciers.

The story of one pigeon, named The King of Rome, has become the stuff of legend. The King of Rome, one of the most famous racing pigeons in Britain, was bred and owned by Charlie Hudson of West Derby. A race from Rome in 1913 was badly disrupted by a storm and, of the 1,000 British birds competing, only two survived.[78] (Belgian birds fared rather better: at least 62 out of 1,200 entrants returned.) The King of Rome flew 1,001 miles from Rome to Derby. The circumstances of his win, against all odds, led to Dave Sudbury writing the song 'The King of Rome' (1983). The first verse highlights the dreams of the ordinary man who aims for the sky or the stars through the exploits of his pigeon. This ordinary pigeon ends up transforming both the life and the spirit of his owner:

In the West End of Derby lives a working man,
He says 'I can't fly but my pigeons can;

And when I set them free, it's just like part of me
Gets lifted up on shining wings.'

'Yeah, I know, but I had to try –
A man can crawl or he can learn to fly;
And if you live round here, the ground seems awful near
Sometimes I need a lift from victory.'[79]

Of course, it is more than just winning, exciting though that may be; for the pigeon fancier, often from blue-collar backgrounds, it is the thrill of the dream, the expectation that they, too, might fly from their troubles and the poverty of their lives.

The pigeon fancier of today is viewed in a respectable light, though this was not always the case. In England, prior to 1858, the year when John Matthews Eaton published his *Treatise on the Art of Breeding and Managing Fancy Pigeons*, they were not held in high regard at all; rather, pigeon fanciers were viewed with suspicion. They were judged to be in the same class as ratcatchers and dog stealers.[80]

How do breeders and racers view their pigeons? As money makers? As supreme athletes? Top fancy pigeon breeder Hayden Bogle once received an offer from the former *Two Fat Ladies* television chef Clarissa Dixon Wright to supply her with pigeons for a friend's restaurant. 'But I couldn't do it,' he said. 'I could never eat a pigeon: they're my friends.'[81]

One pigeon racer spoke of the bond in this way: 'One man, he's got a bird called Carmen – he got it stuffed. That's how close we are with pigeon racing. It's not like, you have a greyhound and when it doesn't finish a race, you shoot it. And when the horse is finished, after winning two races, shoot it and send it to the factory. We don't do that. It's a very personal thing, pigeons.'[82]

Gateway of Dreams, incorporating a statue of *Baron Pierre de Coubertin,* Centennial Olympic Park, Atlanta, Georgia, 1996.

It's interesting to note that Charles Darwin thought the same. He grew so fond of them that he could no longer kill and dissect the birds who had become his companions. In 1860 his daughter Etty's cat entered the pigeon loft and killed some of his pigeons. Darwin had the cat killed, which was out of character for him. Writer Michael Boulter, in his book *Darwin's Garden*, suggests that the reason for this unusual outburst from Darwin was in fact the overwhelming grief he was experiencing at the loss of his favourite daughter, Annie, nine years before, at the age of ten,[83] rather than being a response to the loss of the pigeons, which had been his primary means of research into theories of natural selection and adaptability.

Doves have been part of the opening ceremonies for the Summer Olympic Games, first in 1896, then again in 1920, and in the Olympic Games following. After the cauldron is lit, doves are released as a symbol of peace. The order is important: at the Seoul Games in 1988 the order was reversed, and many looked on in horror as doves still in the area of the cauldron were burned alive as the cauldron was lit. It is interesting to remember that the 1900 Olympics was the first and last Olympics to include live pigeon shooting. If white pigeons had been part of the opening ceremony in 1900, would the link between peace and bloodshed have been made?

Recent events in the United Kingdom have challenged the firmly held belief that pigeon racing can be defined as a sport. Pigeon fanciers have been told that they must pay business rates because their hobby is not a recognized sport. One club wrote to the Queen in her role as Patron of the Royal Pigeon Association. Pigeon fanciers will be forced to pay rates on the sheds where they store their race baskets because they are not officially recognized as a sports club. A spokesperson for HM Revenue and Customs said that pigeon racing was not listed as one of the sports eligible for business rates relief under the Community Amateur Sports Club scheme.[84]

Another blow to the sport came in 2007, when the British Parliament banned pigeon racing from the mainland of continental Europe to Britain because of the risk of avian flu. A Labour Member of the European Parliament, Brian Simpson, supported pigeon fanciers in asking that the bans be lifted, stating that pigeons are a low risk in regard to avian flu.

Another dark side is the 'sport' of pigeon shooting. Pigeon shooting is banned in some countries, where clay pigeons are substituted. In other countries, though, the practice of using live pigeons continues. Pigeons are trapped and taken to gun clubs. In the USA this practice is mostly illegal, but perhaps because they are pigeons, rather than 'cute' animals, this underhand activity is overlooked. Pennsylvania is the last state to permit pigeon shooting. Pigeon poachers illegally trap pigeons in New York. Often the pigeons are starving and barely alive when they arrive at the shooting location. Many are left to die, or

The start of a pigeon race, New York, 1915.

stomped on, or thrown into the garbage. In New York a radical underground movement of concerned citizens has sprung up; they patrol the streets, sabotaging the tactics of pigeon poachers. Only time and education will bring about changes in legislation to protect pigeons from this cruelty.

4 Loved or Loathed: Portrayals in Literature, Art and Culture

Pigeons and doves have inspired artists and writers throughout the centuries. From mosaics and icons to sculpture, poetry, paintings and plays, their presence has been a constant. Sometimes their inclusion in literature is meant to instruct, on other occasions, purely to delight. Because of the relationship we have had with the pigeon for thousands of years, artists have tried to capture its partnership in the sacred, its role as a messenger, and have portrayed the pigeon as a beacon pointing beyond the ordinary, a sign of that elusive ideal for which our hearts long: freedom and peace.

Pigeons or doves in art or literature usually appear for one of four reasons: to provide factual information, to be a symbol or example of love, as an item to hate or loathe, or to be a means of moral instruction. Pigeon/dove is unique in that it roosts at both ends of the range of emotions, from love to hate. This highlights, yet again, the dichotomy between the two.

FACTUAL

In Greek and Roman literature, the pigeon was usually mentioned in order to illustrate the factual. In conversation with Glaucon in Plato's *Republic* (Book v), Socrates refers to selection in the breeding of birds. Aristotle's work has numerous references to

Françoise de Mulder, *Saddam Hussein*, 1990.

هدية
صياغة زينه

pigeons and shows a good knowledge of their characteristics and their habits. In his *History of Animals*, he describes five species of wild pigeon, all of which are known today.[1] In Roman literature, Varro discusses the high prices paid for pigeons in *De rerum rusticarum*. He also noted that they bred all year round except for the month of February; this may be the origin of this fallacy.[2]

Pigeons are mentioned in works by Cato the Elder, Virgil, Pliny and Juvenal (who mentioned the prevalence of pigeons in the attics of Rome). Aelian wrote of their laying habits, noting that pigeons lay two eggs, the first hatched by the male, the second by the female. This, too, is a fallacy.[3]

As mentioned earlier, pigeons played a role in Greek and Roman mythology.[4] In Greek mythology, a dove was the means by which the Argonauts passed through the Symplegades. In

Girl holding dove, sepia photograph, 1902.

1592 the Dutch astronomer and cartographer Petrus Plancius named a star cluster, just outside Canis Major, as Columba (dove). Sometimes the constellation is known as Columba Noachi (referring to the dove in the story of Noah's Ark) rather than Columba with its Greek mythological reference to the Argonaut saga.

Some writers had a deep interest in pigeons and their breeds. Shakespeare was either a breeder of pigeons, or knew breeders,

'The Nicobar Pigeon, drawn from life by George Edwards January AD 1761', from *Gleanings of Natural History*, *III* (London, 1764).

for his writings sometimes describe characteristics of pigeons which would be known only from close observation. In *As You Like It* (IV, 1) Rosalind says to Orlando: 'I will be more jealous of thee than a Barbary cock-pigeon over his hen'. This could be the first time a specific breed of pigeon is noted in English literature. Shakespeare's knowledge of the gentleness of the dove, combined with their strong parental instincts to protect their young, is alluded to in *Henry VI, Part III* (II, 2): 'The smallest worm will turn, being trodden on; and doves will peck, in safeguard of their brood.'

Pendant, c. 1798– 1809, French, gold set with pastes.

Charles Dickens had a sound knowledge of pigeons and particular breeds. He demonstrated this in *Barnaby Rudge*:

> There were more pigeons about the dreary stable yard and out-buildings than anybody but the landlord could reckon up. The wheeling and circling flights of runts, fantails, tumblers, and pouters, were perhaps not quite consistent with the grave and sober character of the building, but the monotonous cooing, which never ceased to be raised by some among them all day long, suited it exactly, and seemed to lull it to rest.[5]

Beatrix Potter's *The Tale of the Faithful Dove*, written in 1907, was based on a true story. It was published in a limited edition after her death. Although it has since been re-issued, Potter never illustrated the manuscript, hence this tale is not well known, even amongst Potter fans. The story tells something of the faithfulness and loyalty of a pigeon-pair. Potter mentions the role of pigeons in the smuggling racket, as well as demonstrating a careful eye to different breeds and to their nesting habits (Potter knows that there is a delay of a day between the laying of the first and the second eggs.) It is a shame that this story is not better known, for its accurate information on the habits of pigeons, the breeds and their part in history alongside humans makes this an informative tale.

We know that pigeons have lived amongst us for thousands of years, easily adapting to the architecture of cities with their many ledges and clifflike structures. These sheltered niches or recesses afford protection for their young. Some city dwellers wonder why no one ever sees a baby pigeon. This question was posed to the late E. B. White:

> Q– I wonder if anyone has ever seen a baby pigeon in New York City?
> A– Yes, cases have been reported. I saw a squab this afternoon in a nest at No. 813 Fifth Avenue, third floor front, a short walk from the men's bar of Carlton House . . . The nest commands a view of the pony ride in Central park, enjoys a fashionable address, and belongs to the baroque school of pigeons' nests.[6]

LOVE: EARTHLY AND DIVINE

For many writers and artists, the attraction of the dove was and still is its association with love and the gentle art of wooing and courtship. For the most part, it is the dove, not the pigeon, who ascends to these dizzy emotional heights. Many artists have expressed this love, or fascination, through literature, music or art. Occasionally this fondness was expressed in another way; in the case of Elizabeth Barrett Browning, noted for her great affection for the dove, one of the most sincere compliments she could pay a friend was to present him with a pair of doves. Her poem 'My Dove' is in part an acknowledgement of the lessons she had learned from her doves:

Vintage postcards portray cultural associations with doves in a number of ways: from being symbols of innocence and purity, to conveying passion or romance.

> So teach ye me the wisest part,
> My little doves! to move
> Along the city ways, with heart
> Assured by holy love,
> And vocal with such songs as own
> A fountain to the world unknown.

Other Victorian poets penned poems which spoke of romantic love. Not surprisingly, Robert Browning compares his love (perhaps Elizabeth?) to a dove: 'How say you? Let us, O my dove, Let us be unashamed of soul . . .'.[7] Tennyson and Wordsworth also associated the dove with romance, Tennyson in 'Locksley Hall', 'The Gardener's Daughter' and 'Maud', and Wordsworth in 'O Nightingale! Thou Surely Art'.

Sometimes the lyrics of love songs compare love with the faithfulness of a dove, as well as describing physical feelings, the

'Dove and Rose',
William Morris
design for curtain
material.

'flutters' associated with romantic love, as flight or feeling able to soar. There is, of course, the fact that in English 'love' rhymes with 'dove', making this a natural and easy association (harder to do with the word 'pigeon'). Examples include popular hits from different eras, including 'On the wings of a dove', based on Psalm 55:1–7 and set to music by Felix Mendelssohn.

Pigeons and doves have been portrayed as aiding seekers of love. In the film *Enchanted* (2007), the protagonist, Princess Giselle, finds herself in modern day New York City, but whereas in the 1950 Disney version of *Cinderella*, small birds, such as sparrows, assist Cinderella in her household chores, in New York large pigeons, the available 'sparrows' of New York, help Giselle instead.

In *Donkey Skin* (Jacques Demy, 1970), a variation of Charles Perrault's *Cinderella*, doves are featured in many scenes. In the courtyard of the palace, the princess is sitting, playing a harpsichord, singing about love. White fantail pigeons surround her; indeed, there are fantails in the majority of scenes with her. Even in her bedroom, there is a small dovecote next to her bed, with many fantails in it and upon it. The doves, symbolizing innocence and purity, highlight dangerous undertones. Unlike the innocence and comedy of *Enchanted*, in *Donkey Skin* the doves reveal a darker theme in the story by symbolizing the innocence of the princess as contrasted with the immorality of her father, who is prepared to break the taboo of incest by seeking to marry her.[8]

Ernst Philippe Zacharie, *Woman with Pigeons*, c. 1883, oil on canvas.

On occasion, writings about the dove indicate a different love: that of God. Sometimes this divine love forces a comparison between God's love and our own love, mirrored in our ethical behaviour. In *Paradise Lost* Milton considers the act of Creation, imagining God brooding like a dove, bringing everything into being. Overwhelmed by a profound sense of awe, Milton calls upon God for help, for this awareness of God's power and goodness acts as a mirror to his soul. Milton knows in his heart that he has fallen short:

> . . . thou from the first
> Wast present, and with mighty wings outspread
> Dove-like sat'st brooding on the vast abyss
> And mad'st it pregnant: what in me is dark
> Illumine, what is low raise and support.[9]

William Blake protested against the custom of keeping caged birds; he argued that it was not only cruel, but it was also against the Divine Plan: 'A dove-house filled with doves and pigeons/ Shudders Hell through all its regions.'[10]

Keats's poem, 'The Dove', is poignant; it contrasts what happened to his dove with the poet's naivety and unintentional cruelty:

> I had a dove, and the sweet dove died;
> And I have thought it died of grieving.
> O, what could it grieve for? its feet were tied,
> With a silken thread of my own hand's weaving.[11]

Several picture books which centre on Christmas include *'Memories of the Manger* by Michelle Medlock Adams, the dove tells the Nativity story. In *The Animals' Christmas Carol* by Helen

Ward, the animals each sing about the gift they gave the Christ Child; in the turtledoves' case, they gave him the gift of song.[12] The theme of gift is addressed in *Thomas and the Dove* by Józef Wilkoń.[13] Thomas shyly presents the Christ Child with a simple, wooden dove that he has made. Thomas is embarrassed, because he has already seen the rich and lavish gifts that have been given to him. As Jesus stretches out his hand to receive the dove, the dove spread its wings and flies upward, alive. The gift has not only been received, but also transformed as a sign of something greater than a simple wooden bird.

The song 'The Twelve Days of Christmas', as familiar as Christmas trees and holly, began its life as a revolutionary idea. Between 1558 and 1829 in England, it was illegal to be Catholic. During those years, when Catholics were forbidden to practice their faith, either publicly or privately, codes were devised in order to teach young Catholics the basis of their faith. One of these memory aids may have been the song 'The Twelve Days of Christmas', which it has been suggested was written as a sung form of the catechism.[14] According to this, the second day, the 'two turtledoves', is an allegory for the Old and New Testaments.

HATE AND PERSECUTION

When did widespread hatred of the humble pigeon become common practice in Western culture? Though pigeon fanciers, or pigeon racers, have not always been viewed as pillars of society, the idea of the pigeon as something that is to be hated and feared, and that therefore warrants elimination, is a relatively recent phenomenon. It has been suggested that Woody Allen's film *Stardust Memories* (1980) was the first recorded instance of the phrase 'rats with wings' being used as a description of feral pigeons.[15] It is unclear whether Allen coined the phrase, but it is the first time it had been used in popular film. In the film, Sandy Bates, played by Allen, panics when a pigeon flies into his apartment. The contrast of opinions is reflected in the reactions of Sandy and Dorrie, played by Charlotte Rampling:

> *Dorrie*: Hey that's so pretty!
> *Sandy*: No, it's not pretty at all, they're . . . they're rats with wings!
> *Dorrie*: No, it's probably a good omen; it'll bring us good luck.
> *Sandy*: No – get it out of here, it's probably one of those killer pigeons.
> *Dorrie*: Let's get it something to eat, to coax it down . . .
> *By this time, Sandy has hold of a fire extinguisher.*
> *Sandy*: See? It's got a swastika on it!

Could this be the reference behind this remark in a book for teenagers:

> And there she was, my special pigeon, hiding in the leaf mould under a hedge.
> . . . 'Is it a rat?' he hissed, backing off.
> 'A rat with feathers?', I tutted at him.[16]

Other terms of derision include 'sky rats', 'sewer eagles' and 'gutter falcons'. Tom Lehrer's satirical song lyrics to 'Poisoning Pigeons in the Park' (1959) suggest an outing to the park to feed the pigeons cyanide-coated peanuts. Whilst there is open dislike of the pigeon, the lyrics address other topics such as courtship and boredom, with the pigeon being a minor character, a catalyst for other events.

The pigeon has been written about in reference to war and persecution. In *The Black Tulip*, Dumas tells the story of Cornelius van Baerle, imprisoned at Loevestein for an alleged political offence against William, Prince of Orange. While in prison, he captures two stray pigeons from Dort, and these pigeons settle

Doves are sometimes used in political satire as symbols of an ideal and of that ideal's downfall. Darwish Ahmad Darwish, *George Bush*.

in his prison cell. They are released with messages which lead to Van Baerle's freedom.

Sometimes the use of the pigeon symbolizes darker forces, as in Isaac Bashevis Singer's short story 'Pigeons', set in Warsaw during the 1930s. Singer's main character, Professor Vladislav Eibeschutz, dies as a result of an injury from anti-Semites. The professor had loved and fed birds, inside and outside his apartment. The pigeons, representing the vulnerable, the easy target, in this case the Jews, are later transformed into a mighty, powerful force. During his funeral procession toward the Old City, pigeons fly overhead. 'Their numbers increased so rapidly that they covered the sky between the buildings on either side of the narrow street and darkened the sky as if during an eclipse. They paused, suspended in the air for a moment, then, in a body, kept pace with the procession by circling around it.'[17]

Perhaps this closing positive reference to the pigeon reflects something of Singer himself, for he loved pigeons. When he walked the New York streets around upper Broadway, carrying a brown paper bag filled with birdseed, the pigeons would fly towards him from several blocks.

Abba Kovner's poem 'My Little Sister' narrates an event that took place during the Holocaust. He writes of his father's attempt to secure a hiding place for his sister within a convent. When she reaches the convent gate, nine nuns meet his sister, standing with doves (the innocent?) eating from their hands, perhaps suggesting protection, or care.[18]

Bernard Gotfryd's Holocaust memoir, *Anton the Dove Fancier*, continues the theme of persecution. Gotfryd tells of watching his neighbour, Anton, who kept pigeons. After the occupation of Poland, Anton is arrested by the Gestapo. The Nazis requisition his pigeons, but when they go to collect them they find that the birds are dead inside the dovecote. Anton is charged

Pablo Picasso,
Dove of Peace,
1949.

with sabotage and sent away. When Gotfryd is sent to the Majdanek concentration camp, he comes across Anton, who is now a kapo. On the last transport out of Majdanek, Anton meets his fate; he is killed by prisoners because of his brutal treatment of them. After the war Bernard returns to his home town, Radom, and meets up with Anton's wife. She admits that he was a brutal man who only ever loved his pigeons, perhaps because they didn't have children. Anton's gentleness was only evident in his treatment of the pigeons, certainly not in the way he treated his wife, or how he dealt with the prisoners under his supervision in Majdanek (with the exception of Gotfryd; he remembered him as the kid who used to watch him fly his pigeons, and therefore helped him with food and clothing). The illustration on the cover of the book is a striking picture of a white dove trapped behind the barbed wire of a concentration camp: innocence, an inability to fly, purity imprisoned by evil.

In another account of internment, tending to the needs of pigeons was conveyed as a transforming experience. In Czech writer Bohumil Hrabel's *I Served the King of England*, the main character, Ditie, a waiter in Prague, is eventually jailed. His daily chore is to feed 200 pairs of abandoned courier pigeons. This task becomes his daily joy, his salvation.[19]

MORAL INSTRUCTION

In Aesop's *Fables*, several tales deal with pigeons and doves to highlight key moral lessons. 'The Decoys and the Doves' illustrates the practice of bird-catching and the role of the 'stool pigeon'. The bird-catcher sets out his net, tying several tame doves to it in order to attract wild doves. The wild doves, seeing the others, fly to them and are snared. When the wild doves notice the bird-catcher, and realize the trick, they are angry with the tame doves; being of the same species, they should have warned them.[20] Another fable, 'The Ant, the Pigeon and the Bird-catcher', addresses the evasion of the bird-catcher by the intervention of the ant, who was rewarding the pigeon's earlier good deed. Other tales mirror the supposed innocence (or gullibility) of the dove (in 'The Doves and the Kite' and 'The Jackdaw and the Doves'), as well as making reference to their (supposed) prolific breeding habits in 'The Dove and the Crow'.

In 'The Canonization', John Donne writes of our complicated selves, the opposing, and perhaps frightening, facets of personality; the dove symbolizes the gentler, peaceful component: 'We are tapers too, and at our own cost die, And we in us find the eagle and the dove . . .'[21]

In T. H. White's *The Sword in the Stone*, certain natural characteristics of the pigeon are noted as qualities worthy of admiration:

Jean-Baptiste Greuze (1725–1805), *Innocence: A Girl with a Dove*, oil on canvas.

'The pigeon,' said Archimedes, 'is a kind of Quaker. She dresses in grey. A dutiful child, a constant lover, and a wise parent, she knows, like all philosophers, that the hand of every man is against her. She has learned throughout the centuries to specialize in escape. No pigeon has ever committed an act of aggression nor turned upon her persecutors; but no bird, likewise, is so skilled in eluding them . . . Vigilant, powdery, odorous and loosefeathered – so that dogs object to take them in their mouths – armoured against pellets by the padding of these feathers, the pigeons coo to one another with true love, nourish their carefully hidden children with true solicitude, and flee from the aggressor with true philosophy . . . They are loving individualists surviving against the forces of massacre only by wisdom in escape.'[22]

Similar qualities are attributed to pigeons in Pam Ayres's children's book, *Bertha and the Racing Pigeon*: 'Bertha was a Wood Pigeon. Not a Great Brain, you might say, but an honest, hardworking person, rather plain and kind.'[23]

In Frank Capra's *Mr Smith Goes to Washington*, newly appointed senator Jefferson Smith (played by James Stewart) takes his pigeons with him to Washington, DC. As he alights from the train, greeted by the sophisticated folk of the nation's capital, he proudly displays and protects his crate of pigeons. As they tease him, asking if the pigeons are going to carry messages back to his mother, he thinks they are being serious, and mentions that he is hoping to enter one of them in the Nationals. Within the film, the pigeons could signify the innocent, the ordinary citizen, like Jefferson Smith; there are no airs or graces, nothing hidden, what you see is what you get. As a pigeon has nothing to hide, its behaviour dictated by genes and nurture, so too, with Smith. As an American citizen, the leaders of the nation have influenced his behaviour, especially the writers of the Constitution and the example of Abraham Lincoln. Smith may be an ordinary man, but he knows how he should act. A pigeon is an ordinary bird, yet it knows how to fly, how to home. It does not go against its nature, and neither does Smith. From the ordinary, extraordinary outcomes occur. As a pigeon can fly long distances, yet still find its way home, Smith can last the distance

Pigeons have remarkable eyesight. They are able to view a 340° field of vision, as well as being able to detect ultraviolet radiation, making for successful navigation.

in hostile conditions until he has found 'home' amongst a flock that will recognize him and see him as one of their own.

In the film *Mary Poppins*, who can forget the poignant figure of the bird lady on the steps of St Paul's Cathedral, surrounded by pigeons? 'Feed the birds, tuppence a bag.' In an interview, Robert B. and Richard M. Sherman, the lyricists, spoke of the significance of the bird lady, saying that she represented more than the mere feeding of pigeons; the song was about caring for the lowliest, the insignificant, and that is part of the charm of the song and the character. Pigeons also figure in the scenes with Bert the chimney-sweep as he draws chalk pictures on the pavement. The pigeons are the onlookers; of his own class (the streets), unnoticed by the well-to-do, but there nonetheless.

French eighteenth-century snuff-box set with enamels of doves, base.

opposite: lid.

In Carlo Collodi's classic, *Pinocchio*, it is a pigeon that comes to the rescue of Pinocchio. It is portrayed as a bird of wisdom, certainly not silly or foolish; that role is Pinocchio's. The Pigeon could be an archetypal wise or holy figure. It 'encounters' the very person/marionette for whom he has been searching (as in many religious tales, or stories of enlightenment). This archetype is continued in its revealing words. On hearing Pinocchio exclaim that one of his least favourite foods is now delicious, the Pigeon, or 'teacher', answers his 'disciple' with a proverb: 'You must remember', answered the Pigeon, 'that hunger is the best sauce!'[24] In the way of the holy (and here I am reminded particularly of Hasidic tales), the Pigeon, after delivering Pinocchio to his destination (or 'destiny') flies away 'not wanting any thanks for a kind deed'.[25]

Within the pages of a series of books for children,[26] following the antics of 'The Pigeon', Mo Willems addressed several early childhood themes such as responsibility and knowing one's limits or boundaries. On Willems's webpage, one of the frequently asked questions is: 'Why did you choose a Pigeon to star in your books?' The answer does not include an explanation of his attraction to pigeons, or the use of the subtext of the invisible in

books for children (who frequently feel they are overlooked, or invisible). No, the answer is quirky: 'A hippopotamus wouldn't fit on the page.'

Three books for teenagers, *Feather Wars, Where Pigeons Go To Die* and *Mister P and His Remarkable Flight,* deal with issues such as isolation, bullying, friendship, change and death. The derision that some feel towards pigeons allows the adolescent to identify with the 'outcast', as well as 'soar' above such limiting labels and prejudices. In *Mister P and His Remarkable Flight,* Vincent, sent away from his parents' drought-stricken farm, befriends a stubborn pigeon, Mister P. Vincent's isolation and loneliness threaten to overwhelm him. Eventually he comes to terms with what it means to have a 'home', and this is mirrored in the story of Mister P, as he fails to make his way 'home' after a number of incidents during a race. As Vincent's family struggles with the destructive nature of the drought, which has caused the family to split up, Mister P's partner and squabs are destroyed by the power of a cat, and he has to live without them. *Feather Wars* examines the theme of war: war within a family and within the local community, as well as battles in the global context, through the way people perceive pigeons. Sam's father volunteers his pigeons for the war effort. At the close of the book, the destroyed pigeons represent the casualties of war, and the sole survivor the strength of the human, endowed with the ability to start afresh. In *Where Pigeons Go To Die*, the grandfather is a pigeon fancier. He talks to his grandson about how he had tried living in the city: 'It wasn't for me anymore. I was domesticated and loved my nest. I was like a pigeon, free to fly away but content to stay at home.'[27] Later, when his grandfather is dying, the ten-year-old grandson takes him from his hospital bed and transports him home on his child's wagon, so that he can die in his 'nest', with his pigeons nearby.

On the Waterfront (1954), directed by Elia Kazan, uses pigeons throughout the film to convey several underlying themes. In the opening scene, Terry Malloy, played by Marlon Brando, triggers an event that has repercussions on how he is portrayed, and by the mob controlling the docks. On his way home, Malloy stops to inform Joey that he has found one of his pigeons. He says he'll take the pigeon up to the loft on the roof. Joey says he'll meet him there. When he arrives, members of the mob push him off the building.

Later in the film, Joey's sister Edie goes up to the roof and meets Terry in his own loft. When she remarks that she is surprised that he is interested in pigeons, Malloy's reply is really a description of his own life, caught in the snares of the mafia:

> *Malloy*: D'you know, this city is full of hawks, that's a fact . . . they hang around on top of big hotels and they spot a pigeon in the park and fly down on them.
> *He brings out one of his birds.*
> He's my lead bird – he's always on top of the perch. You know, if another bum tries to come along and take his place, he really lets him have it.

When Edie comments that 'Even pigeons aren't peaceful', Malloy responds in one of the few tender moments in the film: 'They are very faithful. They get married, just like people, and they stay that way until one of them dies.' When he asks her if she'd like to go and have a beer with him, she is on the outside of the loft, the wire mesh separating not only Terry and Edie from each other, but also creating the divide between two very different worlds.

One evening, she finds him lying on the roof, listening to his pigeons. The mob is closing in, and Malloy is wanted for questioning by the authorities. He says: 'The pigeons . . . they're nervous. There was a hawk around here before.' After he testifies, he goes back to his loft, and finds that all his pigeons have been killed as payback. One of the kids rushes past him, yelling 'A pigeon for a pigeon!' There is still no safe place on the waterfront for pigeons to hide from hawks.

On the Waterfront seems to have influenced Jim Jarmusch's film *Ghost Dog: The Way of the Samurai* (1999). As in *On the Waterfront*, the mafia are involved. The African American mafia hitman known as Ghost Dog models himself after the samurai way or code of life, as outlined in the book of Yamamoto Tsunetomo's recorded sayings, *Hagakure*. Ghost Dog, the retainer of one of the mobsters, communicates with his boss or 'master' via homing pigeons. The opening sequence is an aerial shot of a pigeon and its view of the city as it is airborne. Eventually the pigeon lands on top of a building, near his coop. Ghost Dog, his owner, is reading *The Way of the Samurai*. His intensity is juxtaposed with the calmness of the pigeon; in a sense, the pigeon has found its 'way'. Ghost Dog is trying to master the rules of the samurai, whereas the pigeon has already found its way home. Ghost Dog finds that he has been targeted for death by the mob after the boss's daughter witnesses one of his hits.

In the scene where he kills the boss, the boss is watching a Betty Boop cartoon in which she is trying to catch pigeons with a large net. In comes Ghost Dog, to 'catch' one, but his 'net' turns out to be faulty. When the mob realizes that the only connection to him is via pigeons, they embark on random shooting sprees on rooftop pigeon lofts. Eventually they target the correct one, and Ghost Dog returns home to find that all of his pigeons have been killed except one (reminiscent of the scene in *On The Waterfront)*. A dead pigeon has been placed on the bed (a reference to the scene in *The Godfather* with the horse's head in the bed). The remaining pigeon delivers a message to the mob from Ghost Dog: 'Even if the samurai's head were to be suddenly cut off he should still be able to perform one more action with certainty.' Ghost Dog's remaining task is to kill the entire mob, with the exception of his boss and the boss's daughter, in retaliation for the death of his pigeons. At the close of the film, when Ghost Dog is gunned down by his boss, the solitary pigeon flies down and sits with him as he dies. As Ghost Dog remained faithful to his master, the pigeon has remained loyal to its owner. Earlier in the film Ghost Dog read: 'According to what one of the elders said, taking an enemy is like a hawk taking a bird.' The hawk has struck.[28]

OTHER CULTURAL CONNECTIONS

Within the fanfare of the magical, or the fantastic, the magician is a frequent inhabitant, with doves flying out of his hat, or coming out of his or her coat sleeve. Perhaps this sense of the mysterious will always be an undercurrent within the Magic Circle. Why are pigeons or doves associated with magicians? They are clever birds, easily trained and hardy – one does not need to be as vigilant in terms of avoiding draughts and weather changes

Ghost Dog, mastering *The Way of the Samurai*, rests among his beloved pigeons. *Ghost Dog* (1999).

as for some other birds. Their homing instincts, if the birds do get out, come into play, and they bond with their owners. The pigeon/dove is one of the characters in Colin Thompson's *The Great Montefiasco*.[29] The Great Montefiasco, the worst magician in the world, does have pigeons as part of his act, as is common with magicians, but unlike the familiar white doves appearing from the magician's hat, when he coughs, two scruffy pigeons fall out of his coat sleeves. They are the common rock pigeon, found on the streets in cities the world over. The illustrations depict the pigeons perching on the back of chairs, drinking in the bar after a show and sleeping in the top drawer of his bedside table. It's a real switch from the way we usually perceive magicians and their white doves. It is a holding up of the mirror so that we can see magicians for who they really are: ordinary people with props.

Pigeons have devotees from all parts of society. Many famous people have been pigeon fanciers: Mary, Queen of Scots, who kept turtledoves, W. S. Gilbert, Monet (the pigeon loft is still in Monet's garden at Giverny), Roy Rogers, Yul Brynner, Elvis Presley, Guccio Gucci (who paid $10,000 for one bird), Willi

Mike Tyson and dove.

Brandt, the former chancellor of West Germany, and Mike Tyson. There is something quite moving when examining a photograph of Tyson holding a dove in his hands; this boxer, associated with violence in both his public and private lives, is gently holding a small bird, a symbol of peace. Tyson is quoted as saying: 'This is my next love, after my kids. They're very soothing.' Pigeons may inadvertently have been the reason behind Tyson's boxing career. As a child, Tyson kept pigeons. When he was eleven years old a boy killed one of his beloved pigeons. Tyson, who had never shown great anger before, exploded and hit the offender over and over again. From then on, he trained for a career in boxing. He still keeps pigeons, and at the time of writing has about 350.[30]

Percy to the Rescue describes an ordinary rock pigeon living in London, exploring the city sights and ending up being given a royal roost at Buckingham Palace.[31] Although a work of fiction, there is a grain of truth within this tale, for the British Royal Family has an interest in pigeons and pigeon racing as a result of a gift of racing pigeons from King Leopold II of Belgium in 1886. The loft is kept at Sandringham Palace. In 1990 one of the Queen's pigeons took part in the Pau race, coming first in the Section 5th Open.[32] At one time, the royal pigeons had a better record of wins than the royal racehorses. There is also a dove on the sceptre known as the Rod of Equity and Mercy that is carried by the English monarch during the coronation ceremony.

Doves and pigeons have featured in works of art from the religious to the modern, including those by Picasso, Chagall and Magritte. Some artists kept doves, including Picasso and Matisse. Picasso's *Child Holding a Dove* shows his search for a new direction, coming at the end of the summer of 1901. His subjects receive his sympathy; in this painting both child and

Pablo Picasso, *Child with a Dove,* 1901, oil on canvas.

René Magritte, *The Healer*, gouache on paper, 1936.

dove are painted with a compassionate eye. Picasso's fondness for doves was reflected in the choice of name for his daughter, Paloma, which is Spanish for 'dove'. Picasso said of his birds:

> These are really birds for a philosopher. All human utterance has its stupid side. Fortunately I have the turtledoves to make fun of me. Each time I think I'm saying something particularly intelligent, they remind me of the vanity of it all.[33]

The Surrealist René Magritte used doves in a number of his paintings to convey a range of themes and symbols. Indeed, it has been said: 'if you look long enough you can always find a Dove in Magritte.'[34] *Le Thérapeute* (*The Healer*) depicts a seated figure. There is a cage where the body and head should be, and within the cage are two doves. *La Magie noire* (*Black Magic*) represents a naked woman/statue, painted partly in blue. There are a number of versions, in which the statue is shown in the process of transforming itself into a woman, or vice versa. In a version from 1945, for example, there is a white dove/pigeon on her shoulder. Perhaps in this instance the dove represents innocence and/or purity. *Les Heureux présages* (*The Good Omen*) is bright and optimistic: a large white dove, flecked with gold, flies through the air with flowers as its tail feathers. *La Grande Famille* (*The Large Family*) has a giant pigeon in it, and *L'idole* (*The Idol*) a large dove that dominates the sky.

Doves are sometimes part of wedding and funeral services, and are known as 'release' birds. Pigeons are released at the close of the wedding as a symbol of love, purity and loyalty. At funerals, the birds represent the soul's final journey, as well as signifying an awareness or acknowledgement of something greater than ourselves. The doves fly upwards, towards heaven, on a new journey. Doves are part of other special events, including the Commonwealth Games, and the annual remembrance service at Hiroshima, where 1,000 doves are released each year.

Western culture, and with it the Western psyche, is confused about the pigeon/dove. On the one hand, reference is made to our sweethearts as 'doves', we buy Valentine's Day cards or Christmas cards heavily embossed with white doves, and we recognize them as symbols of peace. On the other hand, pigeons are hated, viewed as rodents, 'rats with wings' and in some places their activities are severely curtailed.

Consider the contrasting situations in Venice and in London with reference to the care of pigeons in the public domain. Pigeons have been an accepted part of the Venetian landscape since 1204, when the pigeon was officially sanctioned by the

Pigeons in Trafalgar Square.

Doge Enrico Dandolo for its role in relaying a message from Constantinople during the Fourth Crusade. Provision has been made in the courtyard of the Doge's palace for pigeons with the installation of stone drinking bowls. Some suggest that the Venetians have accepted the pigeon because of the flight of the white doves around Piazza di San Marco during Holy Week (representing the Holy Spirit). Regardless of the reason, pigeons have become one of Venice's mascots, and are highly protected and treasured. For many years the hundreds of pigeon were fed by the city; they were readily accepted as the city's responsibility. During the 1950s, however, an insurance company, Assicurazioni Generali, took on this privilege, perhaps as a marketing strategy.[35] The story is changing; recent reports speak of the city trying to stop the sale of birdseed to tourists in order to decrease the number of pigeons. This measure is intended to stop pigeon droppings from damaging the ancient paving of the piazza.

In 2000 London's Mayor, Ken Livingstone, described pigeons as 'rats with wings' and declared war on the world-famous Trafalgar Square pigeons. One measure introduced was to ban the sale of corn on the Square, a method intended to starve the pigeons (an estimated 4,000 birds were in the flock). The Greater London Authority (GLA) withdrew a licence from Bernie Rayner, whose family had sold bird food on Trafalgar Square for the past 50 years. Other methods used included the introduction of hawks to kill the pigeons, water hoses and industrial hoovers. These actions sparked the formation of a lobby group, Save the Trafalgar Pigeons, with its own website, which helped raise funds in order to feed the birds, fight legal battles, and inform and educate the general public about pigeons in general, and more specifically, what to do if you found an injured one. In February 2007 London outlawed the feeding of pigeons in Trafalgar Square.

Perhaps the difference in attitude can be explained in part with reference to location and significance. Trafalgar Square is not a holy site; therefore the pigeons/doves do not symbolize the Holy Spirit, or particular religious beliefs, and without this sanction can be viewed as pests. Would perceptions change if Trafalgar Square were a sacred place?[36]

5 Exploitation or Conservation: Our 'Feathered Conscience'

Among the species of pigeon or dove that have become extinct since 1600, the most famous are the dodo and the passenger pigeon.

THE DODO

In *Alice's Adventures in Wonderland*, the Dodo is presented as an intelligent figure. After a group of weird and wet bedraggled creatures attempt to dry themselves, the Dodo suggests a race to help them dry off. After the race the question is asked: 'But who has won?'

> This question the Dodo could not answer without a great deal of thought, and it stood for a long time with one finger pressed upon its forehead (the position in which you usually see Shakespeare, in the picture of him), while the rest waited in silence. At last the Dodo said '*Everybody* has won, and *all* must have prizes.'[1]

Many have thought the dodo to be a mythical figure, a character confined to fantasy and legend; for some it is a shock to discover that the dodo was a real bird, related to the pigeon, and extinct by 1681 due to the brutality of humans. The saying

John Tenniel, 'The Dodo', from Lewis Carroll's *Alice's Adventures in Wonderland*.

'as dead as a dodo' means 'long since dead and forgotten'. The dodo didn't win, and never received a prize.

The dodo (*Raphus cucullatus*) once lived on the island of Mauritius. The early explorers of Mauritius called this large dove many names: a wild turkey, a 'hooded swan', a 'bastard ostrich', a booby or a cassowary.[2] The dodo was named either by the Portuguese or by the Dutch sailors that followed them to Mauritius. One school of thought holds that the name came from the sound of its call.[3] Others suggest that it is from the Dutch *dod-aarse* (lump arse).[4] The Portuguese word *doudo* means 'silly'. Sometimes we think of someone as stupid, and call him/her 'a dodo'. This large, flightless dove, the size of a turkey, resided on an island that had no mammals, no predators; it was only with the arrival of humans, mainly the Portuguese, that the dodo faced danger. It was an odd looking bird, with a round body, light and dark grey feathers, yellow legs and a hooked bill. They were about three feet in height, with small wings and bare skin around the eye area, and they weighed in at about fifty pounds. Their tails had curly feathers, like a small plumage. Recent research has challenged the traditional image of the dodo as an overweight bird that would drag its belly across the ground. Measurements of its skeleton at Oxford University, plus bones in collections in the Cambridge Zoology Museum and the

Engraving from H. E. Strickland and A. G. Melville's *The Dodo and its Kindred* (1848), after a painting attributed to Roelandt Savery, late 1620s.

London Natural History Museum, have been used to calculate what its weight might have been. Findings point to a much sleeker bird; if the dodo had been large, its skeleton would not have been able to support its body mass: 'The new reconstruction of the dodo is much thinner and looks more like the first contemporary drawings of the bird.'[5]

Along with other birds, the dodo provided the crews of European ships with ready food and sport, although it was reported to be tough and taste unpleasant. Once the island became a Dutch colony, settlers brought with them the added dangers of domestic animals such as dogs and cats, along with monkeys, rats and pigs. The dogs attacked the adult birds, whilst the other animals tended to concentrate on the eggs and chicks. By 1680 the dodo was extinct.

Dodos were a product of their time; they became extinct because of the conditions of the day; if they had survived a little longer, things may have been different for them. Errol Fuller proposed the following:

> Had dodos survived for a few more decades, colonies might have established themselves in European parks and gardens; they were probably hardy enough creatures. Today, dodos might be as common as peacocks in ornamental gardens the world over! Instead, all that remains are a few bones and pieces of skin, a collection of pictures of varying quality, and a series of written descriptions enormously expressive of the age in which they were conceived yet curiously inadequate in the information they convey.[6]

There were three other giant doves in the family Raphidae, including two varieties of Solitaire, which lived on the islands of

Réunion and Rodriguez. In 1708 François Leguat described the Solitaire in his memoirs:

> The Females are wonderfully beautiful, some fair, some brown; I call them fair, because they are of the colour of fair Hair. They have a sort of Peak, like a Widow's upon their Beak, which is of a dun colour . . . The Feathers on their Thighs are round like shells at one end, and being there very thick, have an agreeable effect. They have two Risings on the Craws, and the Feathers are whiter there

'The Solitaire of Rodriguez', after the engraving in François Leguat, *Voyages et Aventures* (1708), showing a female.

than the rest, which lively represents the fine bosom of a Beautiful Woman. They walk with so much stateliness and good Grace, that one cannot help admiring and loving them.[7]

Leguat also wrote of their mating rituals and dances, as well as the clapping of their wings against their bodies, 'like a rattle'. Leguat wrote about an annual ritual, which he termed the 'betrothal ceremony':

Some days after the young one leaves the nest a Company of 30 or 40 brings another young one to it; and the new-fledged Bird with its Father and Mother joyning with the Band, march to some bye Place. We frequently followed them, and found that afterwards the old ones went each their way alone, or in Couples, and left the two young ones together, which we call a *Marriage*.[8]

Leguat's descriptions met with resistance; people did not believe him. It wasn't until two centuries later that his accounts were taken seriously, due to archaeological finds proving much of what he had written to be true.[9] Once his findings had been substantiated, then the assumption was made that the rest of Leguat's work must be factual as well.

Others wrote of the beautiful, graceful Solitaire, observing that they pine when they are in captivity, and 'When caught they make no sound, but shed tears.'[10] Exquisite writings about this large, gentle dove did not save it from the dangers of the human (unlike the dodo, the Solitaire's flesh was edible). The Rodriguez Solitaire (Raphidae *Pezohaps solitarius*) was extinct by 1800. The Réunion Solitaire (*Ornithaptera solitarius*) was hunted for food and became extinct by 1700.

'The White Dodo',
Victoriornis
imperialis.

There is no archaeological evidence to support that another bird, the Raphidae *Victoriornis imperialis* (known as the white dodo of Réunion), once existed. Instead there are two eyewitness descriptions and a number of paintings. These unusual 'testimonies' to the existence of the white dodo managed to hold enough weight to convince scientists that they had existed. In a painting completed in 1680, Pieter Withoos portrays the white dodo as short, with yellow wings, a bluish tinge on its white plumage, and a high arched tail. The legs and feet were ochre, the nails were black, and the eyelid bright red.[11] Several made it to Europe alive, transported as curios. In 1638 Sir Hamon L'Estrange visited one that was on show in London. He saw

> a great fowl, somewhat bigger than the largest Turkey Cock . . . but stouter and thicker and of a more erect state . . . The keeper called it a Dodo, and in the end of a chymney in the chambers there lay a heape of large pebble

stones, whereof hee gave it many in our sight, some as big as nutmegs and the keeper told us she eats them (conducing to digestion).[12]

Dodos did eat stones, in the manner that pigeons and doves eat grit and small pebbles, to help break down nuts and seeds. The stones were not part of their diet, but tools to aid digestion. The white dodos were hardy birds; they had to have been to have survived the sea voyage to Europe. It is yet another source of shame to learn that this hardiness did not extend to their relations with humans; the white dodo was extinct by 1770.

In Mauritius the tambalacoque tree (*Calvaria major*) is known as the dodo tree. These trees are scarce, facing extinction, like their namesake. The tambalacoque tree was quite common during the time of the dodo. Stories abound that the dodo liked to eat the seeds; as its gastric juices softened the seed, this allowed the seed to germinate when the dodo eventually excreted it. Whether this theory is correct or not, it is fascinating to propose a link between the extermination of one (the dodo) and the scarcity of the other (the tambalacoque). David Day calls this 'one of the most mysterious symbiotic relationships between plant and animal.'[13]

The dodo is used as the symbol for the Jersey Wildlife Preservation Trust, now known as the Durrell Wildlife Conservation Trust, which was set up by Gerald Durrell in 1958. On an expedition to Mauritius, Durrell mused:

It was somehow ironical that we, the flightless mammals, were landing, in one of the biggest flying edifices known on earth, on the area of land that covered the remains of one of the earth's strangest flightless birds; for the Dodo's graveyard, from which were extracted the bones on which our tenuous knowledge of the Dodo is based, lies beneath the tarmac of Plaisance airport.[14]

THE PASSENGER PIGEON (*ECTOPISTES MIGRATORIUS:* 'WANDERING WANDERER')

The now extinct passenger pigeon was once the most abundant land bird on this planet. It made up 25 to 40 per cent of the total land bird life in what became known as the USA: 'Historians and biologists have estimated that 3 to 5 billion Passenger Pigeons populated eastern and central North America at the time of the European Conquest.'[15] Billions of birds darkened the sky, their sound like thunder as they passed overhead. In the eastern USA, they outnumbered all other species of North American birds combined.[16]

They thrilled the early explorers. In his writings Christopher Columbus writes about a type of dove quite unlike the ones he had seen in Europe. He notes they flew in large flocks, so many that they almost blocked out the sun.[17] On 1 July 1534 Jacques Cartier wrote about having seen flocks on what is now Prince Edward Island.[18]

Passenger pigeons flew either close to the ground, or high up, either in a single level, or seeming to be stacked in layers. They flew up to 60 miles an hour, and could continue to fly for hours at a time. Audubon once wrote about a flight of passenger pigeons which took three days to pass. 'Passenger pigeon' derives from the French word 'passager', to pass by. Audubon compared the dark wrought by the pigeons to 'the dark of an eclipse'.

They were beautiful birds, with blue-grey heads and backs. The wings were sometimes spotted with black patches. The chest colour for the males faded to white near their bellies. Their bills were black, legs and feet red, with long tails and red eyes. Their neck feathers were of purple, gold, yellow and green. Thoreau wrote of their beauty: 'this dry slate color, like weather-stained wood . . . [was a] fit color for this aerial traveller, a more subdued and earthy blue than the sky, as its field (or path) is between the sky and the earth.'[19] Commenting on their iridescent neck feathers, he exclaimed: 'The reflections from their necks were very beautiful, they made me think of shells cast up on a beach.'[20]

Adults moulted once a year; the young acquired their adult colours a year after their birth. They bred from April to June, primarily in the north-eastern USA, northern Canada and the Midwest. Their breeding grounds could extend up to 850 square miles. This large nesting area was in Wisconsin, and included about 135 million birds.[21] They took three days to attend to courtship rituals and copulation. Many of their rituals were the same as for other pigeons, but there was one great difference. Sometimes the pigeons would rush and put their wings across the wings of their mate, like a hug. This was not found in other pigeon courtship behaviour, and if a passenger pigeon paired up with another species of pigeon in captivity and this action was performed, it tended to scare the other pigeon rather than enhancing the courtship advances. [22]

The female laid one egg, unlike most other species of pigeon which lay two eggs, and it was incubated for thirteen days. Like most other species of pigeon, the male and female took turns sitting on the nest and gathering food. After the squabs were hatched, they stayed in the nest for two weeks and then were left to their own devices. After a few days they would fly off in a massive flock. The noise of the flock, the bird calls and the beating of their wings, could be heard up to three miles away. The roosting areas attracted predators, including humans. Native American Indians would hunt the passenger pigeons, for they

Passenger Pigeon, lithograph by Robert Havell, after John James Audubon, from *Birds of America* (Philadelphia, 1840–44).

would use their meat, feathers and fat. Unlike the white settlers, they would only hunt what was needed for their subsistence, or later, what was needed for trading purposes. Some tribes would threaten white settlers who killed nesting adults.

Photograph from the old Court House Museum, Vicksburg, Mississippi, of a 'dove of peace' button from the time of the Civil War.

The Indian tribes had different names for the passenger pigeon: *o-me-me-nog* for the Potawatomi, and *omimi* to the Algonquin, both names echoing the sounds the birds made.[23] Other tribes described them in more poetic terms; the Narragansett called them *wuscowhan* (wanderer) and the Choctaw, *putchee nashoba* (lost dove).[24] Passenger pigeons played a part in native ritual and legend; the Hurons, like many other peoples, linked the birds to death, with the souls of the dead coming back in the form of a pigeon. For the Micmacs, the passenger pigeon has a role in the constellation, and is one of the stars between the Big Dipper and the Northern Crown, one of the birds pursuing a bear.[25]

White settlers also held beliefs about the passenger pigeon. In Longfellow's *Evangeline*, reference is made to the passenger pigeon, linking it with death:

> Then it came to pass that pestilence fell on the city,
> Presaged by wondrous signs, and mostly by flocks of wild
> pigeons,
> Darkening the sun in their flight, with nought in their
> craws but an acorn.

One settler, Cotton Mather, held a bizarre notion that when the pigeons disappeared after roosting, they would 'repair to some undiscovered satellite accompanying the earth at a near distance.'[26] One superstition held by the women was that if you buried a male passenger pigeon in the garden, the flowers would be brighter.[27]

The birds fed on nuts or mast,[28] as well as berries, seeds and small insects. They became nomadic because the trees produced nuts of differing amounts at different times during the year, and at different locations. Passenger pigeons were big eaters, perhaps to ward off times of hunger. Sometimes their crops[29] were so crammed with food that they enlarged to the size of an orange. The crops could take in about an eighth of a pint of mast; a crop's contents could reveal large amounts: 17 acorns in one, 104 corn kernels in another, half a pint of beech nuts in another.[30] Passenger pigeons also had the unendearing habit of vomiting if they found something else they would rather eat.[31]

Farmers employed various scare tactics, such as scarecrows and bells, finally resorting to the gun. Farmers could lose crops, as the Plymouth colonists did in 1643. In Canada the 'heavies' of the church were brought in, for pressure was brought to bear by a bishop to excommunicate the pigeons because of crop damage.[32]

Passenger pigeons became a much needed source of food in the country, on the frontier and in the cities. Cookbooks were published that included recipes for passenger pigeons: in pies, as potted pigeon, they were broiled, roasted, smoked, salted or even pickled. In the cities they became an elegant dish for the household or for the restaurant. The *Niles Republican*, a newspaper based in Berrien County, Michigan, published this short poem about the passenger pigeon:

When I shoot my rifle clear,
To pigeons in the skies,
I'll bid farewell to pork and beans,
And live on good pot pies.[33]

The demand for passenger pigeons for the table did not become a problem until the middle of the nineteenth century.

With the development of the railroad, and with the assistance of the telegraph, hunters increased to thousands of men who would descend on nesting colonies and kill the birds. They would be delivered quickly to the cities via rail. In 1860 30,000 miles of track meant that pigeons could be delivered to major destinations very quickly.[34] The numbers of pigeons shipped were incredible. The 1851 nesting at Plattsburgh, New York, yielded 1.8 million pigeons; in 1883 Monroe County, Wisconsin, yielded 2 million.[35]

There were two chief hunting methods: netting and shooting. The grounds were cleared of vegetation and treated grain (sometimes soaked in whiskey) spread on the ground. Stool pigeons were used as decoys and their eyelids were sewn together. In the field they were set on a perch several feet from the ground. They wore booties of skin, and attached to these was a rope. When the rope was loosened, the perch would fall and so would the pigeon. The movement by the pigeon appeared to the wild passenger pigeons as though it was one of their own,

Engraving from *The Illustrated Sporting and Dramatic News*, 3 July 1875.

landing first. When the trappers saw a flock, they would release the stool pigeon as well as several other pigeons known as 'fliers'; these pigeons were attached to a long rope and 'flew' in the air to attract the flock.[36] Large nets were thrown over the pigeons as they were about to land, and then the nets were weighted down to keep them on the ground. Sometimes nets were placed across pigeon flight paths, or near places where they roosted; at night the roosting pigeons would be guided into the nets by torches and stones. Audubon has vividly described some of these trappings. He writes of the organized killing of huge numbers of passenger pigeons that he witnessed at Green River, Kentucky:

> Suddenly there burst forth a general cry of 'Here they come!' The noise which they made, though yet distant, reminded me of a hard gale at sea, passing through the rigging of a close-reefed vessel. As the birds arrived and passed over me, I felt a current of air that surprised me. Thousands were soon knocked down by the pole-men. The birds continued to pour in. The fires were lighted, and a magnificent, as well as wonderful and almost terrifying, sight presented itself. The Pigeons, arriving by the thousands, alighted everywhere, one above another, until solid masses as large as hogsheads were formed on the branches, all round. Here and there the perches gave way under the weight with a crash, and falling to the ground, destroyed hundreds of birds beneath, forcing down the dense groups with which every stick was loaded. It was a scene of uproar and confusion. I found it quite useless to speak, or even to shout to those persons who were nearest to me. Even the reports of the guns were seldom heard, and I was made aware of the firing only by seeing the shooters reloading.[37]

'Passenger Pigeon', aquatint from William Daniell, *Interesting Selections from Animated Nature*, II (London, 1809).

Most trappers would kill the birds by breaking their necks or skulls: 'This could go on for long hours, leaving hands so sore the fingers couldn't move.'[38] The pigeons' fear of blood or seeing feathers meant that the trappers and netters had to clean their equipment thoroughly in between trappings.

Success at capturing birds led to the establishment of another industry: trapshooting. Live pigeons were sold as contest targets. Trapshooting contests resulted in a huge loss of life. In 1881 a contest on Coney Island resulted in the death of over 20,000 birds.[39] 'In one competition, a participant had to kill 30,000 birds just to be considered for a prize.'[40] The most famous character of the trapshooting circuit was Captain Adam H. Bogardus, who once killed 500 pigeons in 528 minutes, loading his own gun.[41] It was a cruel sport; many were mutilated before being released, to make them more 'flighty'. They had been transported in cramped cages, without water. When they arrived at their destination, water was offered and many died in the rush to drink. Some 50,000 birds could be used for a weekly trapshooting competition.

Pigeons have been subjects of art; even skeletal remains can be transformed into something quite beautiful. This photograph hearkens back to its origins, the archaeopteryx.

These cruel practices were noted and, after seven years of lobbying, Henry Bergh, founder of the American Society for the Prevention of Cruelty to Animals, was successful in having trap-shooting banned in New York. Due to public support, trapshooting was banned by the late 1880s.[42] Pennsylvania is the only state openly to host multiple pigeon shoots, mostly held at private gun clubs. Efforts to pass a statewide ban on pigeon shooting in

1999 failed in the Pennsylvania Legislature. At the time of writing, there is intense lobbying by a number of animal welfare groups and concerned citizens to have pigeon shooting outlawed in Pennsylvania. As a comparison, pigeon shooting was banned in Great Britain in 1921.

The number of passenger pigeons declined throughout the 1870s and '80s. As their numbers decreased, so did their breeding, as the pigeons became scared or timid around humans. By 1886 there were only two flocks of pigeons left, one in Pennsylvania and the other in Oklahoma.[43] The passenger pigeon was too popular as a source of food and as an easy target for shooting practice. It became extinct in the wild in 1900. Protective laws came too late to save this magnificent bird.

The last documented wild passenger pigeon was shot on 24 March 1900 by fourteen-year-old Press Clay Southworth on his family's farm near Sargents, Ohio. When the family realized that the bird was a passenger pigeon, they took it to an amateur taxidermist, who stuffed it, substituting shoe buttons for glass eyes. The bird, named Buttons, is on the display in the Ohio Historical Center's museum in Columbus. The date on display is 'March 12' but, according to meticulous research by Christopher Cokinos, this date is incorrect.[44]

Southworth spoke about Buttons to interested members of his family, but it was not until the late 1960s that he started to realize the enormity of the consequences of his actions all those years ago. In an interview Mary Kruse, Southworth's daughter, noted that it wasn't until reading an article about passenger pigeons, which made reference to the boy who had shot the last wild passenger pigeon, printed in the 1968 February/March issue of *Modern Maturity* magazine, that the penny dropped. After reading the article, Southworth wrote an article to the editor describing the event; unfortunately the magazine did not

'Buttons', the last wild passenger pigeon.

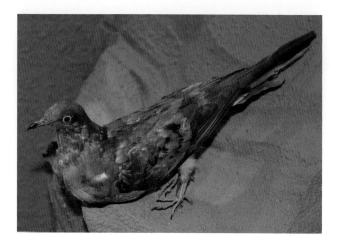

print his letter. Titled 'The Little Boy now 82 yrs old Tells his Story', the letter is Southworth's memory of the events of 24 March 1900:

> On the date in question I was feeding cattle in the barn yard when I saw a strange bird feeding on loose grains of corn near the cattle and as I approached it flew into a large tree near by. I had been raised on a farm and was quite familiar with the various species of wild birds. However this bird was larger than a [Mourning] dove and its flight was quite different than a dove or pigeon [Rock Dove]. I hurried to the house, told my Mother about this strange bird . . . After considerable persuasion she gave me out our 12 guage [*sic*] shot gun with one shell. I was pretty handy with a gun as I had hunted with my older brothers. I found the bird perched high in the tree and brought it down without much damage to its appearance. When I took it to the house Mother

exclaimed – 'It's a passenger pigeon.' She had seen thousands of them when she was a small girl.[45]

On 15 November 1949 a radio play was aired on a local Columbus station. The 15-minute play was about the passenger pigeon, and was called *The Passenger Pigeon – A Lesson in Conservation*. The characters included Indians, pioneers, hunters and residents. Then Buttons speaks, with this bizarre conclusion:

See? I told you I was important and that I could tell quite a story. I'm back on my shelf at the Museum now. And I like it very much. I feel that I have a mission in life. The door is opening now and I believe some children are coming in to look at me. I hope lots of children come here to the Museum to see me because I like children and I know that when they look at me they think about conservation and all it means to our country. So come and see me. I'll be watching for you.[46]

Isn't there something quite odd going on here? A bird, now dead and her species extinct due to the actions of a boy, stating that she likes children and likes being confined to a museum? The voice of a wild passenger pigeon, speaking of the benefits of extinction and the advantages of confinement? A chilling sadness pervades these cheerfully uttered words.

Two passenger pigeons were donated to the newly established Cincinnati Zoo in 1874, before it officially opened the facility to the public in 1875. Several years later, another passenger pigeon was born. She was named after America's First Lady, Martha Washington. The date and year of Martha's birth remain uncertain due to a number of different stories that circulated from the zoo's owner, Sol Stephan, and his son, Joseph.

Sometimes the stories stated that Martha had been purchased from outside the zoo; on other occasions that she had been born at the zoo (which served to enhance the zoo's name and reputation). In 1963 there was a fire at the zoo, and files that may have contained evidence for the correct version of Martha's origin, were destroyed.[47]

Martha lived with several other passenger pigeons, but by 1909 there were only three pigeons left. In April that year one of the two male pigeons died, leaving Martha and George. This was the last known pair of passenger pigeons. In July of the following year, George died, committing Martha to a solitary existence. George's body was not preserved, for his plumage was in a 'poor state'. Once people realized that Martha was the last remaining passenger pigeon, interest rose. The New York Zoo wished to

Martha, the last passenger pigeon.

purchase her, but Sol Stephan refused to part with Martha. She was now a great attraction; visitors flocked to the zoo for one last glimpse before the species became extinct. It's ironic that the region where Martha was confined had been the origin of the first trapshooting club in the USA, and the targets had been passenger pigeons.[48] The surrounding hills and sky had once been thick with passenger pigeon flocks; now they had been reduced to one last female passenger pigeon, confined to captivity. Martha's wings drooped, and her movements were few; this irritated some of the visitors. It got to the point that 'on Sundays we would rope off the cage to keep the public from throwing sand at her to make her walk around.'[49]

When Martha began to moult in the summer of 1914, her feathers were collected and stored. Her keepers, unable to save the species by breeding, were at least alert enough to know that when Martha died, her body should be kept for posterity, and these feathers would be needed for the full portrait.

Martha's final hours are clouded in legend, as are her beginnings. Some reports state that she died alone at about 1pm on Tuesday, 1 September 1914. This tends to be the more readily accepted statement. Sol and Joseph Stephan, however, state that she died at 5pm, and that they were with her when she took her last breath. Perhaps this was another fabrication to paint the zoo and its keepers and operators in the best light. When the leader of the National Audubon Societies, T. Gilbert Pearson, received a telegram informing him of the death of Martha, the last passenger pigeon, he commented that her death 'is a calamity of as great importance in the eyes of naturalists as the death of a kaiser to Germans throughout the world.'[50]

Martha's autopsy was performed by the physician and ornithologist R. W. Shufeldt. During the autopsy, Shufeldt decided not to dissect the heart; he preferred to keep Martha's heart

A statue of Martha stands guard at the entrance to the Cincinnati Zoo, the place of her demise.

whole 'to preserve it in its entirety . . . as the heart of the last "Blue Pigeon" that the world will ever see alive.'[51] Shufeldt's autopsy notes include his own musings about extinction, and whether people seeing Martha, the last passenger pigeon, on display, would heighten work for conservation: 'In due course, the day will come when practically all of the world's avifauna will have become utterly extinct . . . Such a fate for it is coming to pass now, with far greater rapidity than most people realize.'[52]

In 1976 a bronze statue of a passenger pigeon was unveiled at the Cincinnati Zoo, after renovation work on the aviary was complete. The statue forms part of the path that leads to the large wooden doors of the aviary, decorated with reliefs of other extinct and endangered birds. Martha is now also available for scientific research as a three-dimensional image on the Smithsonian website. This means she can be studied, but not touched, to save on wear and tear.

This is a sorry chapter in the history of extermination and exploitation. Although several theories have been proposed as to why the passenger pigeon became extinct in such a short time, including a rise in disease, depletion of forests, an inability to breed as numbers decreased, abandonment of nests after hunters had taken the squabs, and perhaps a preference for huge colonies, the main reason was destruction at the hand of humans. In this age when we can make new inventions, discover other galaxies and find cures for diseases, we have allowed, to our shame, the passenger pigeon to 'pass by' forever.

Other pigeons that have become extinct include the Pigeon Hollandaise (*Alectroenas nitidissima,* or the Mauritius Blue

Rodrigues Solitaires,
Pezophaps solitaria.

Pigeon) in 1826, the Bonin Wood Pigeon (Columbidae *Columba versicolor*), last seen in 1889, and the beautiful Choiseul Crested Pigeon (Columbidae *Microgoura meeki*) from the Solomon Islands. We only know of its existence because of A. S. Meeks, an Australian who, in 1904, collected six specimens of this pigeon from a trader in a village.[53] Expeditions led by experienced ornithologists, part of the Whitney South Sea Expedition of the American Museum in 1927 and 1929, failed to find any of these pigeons. The island's inhabitants told the expedition that the introduction of cats had led to their destruction.

In the New Hebrides, on the island of Tanna, lived the Tanna Dove (Columbidae *Gallicolumba ferruginea*). Little is known about this dove, except from notes and illustrations made by the naturalist Johann Reinhold Forster and his son, who were attached to one of Cook's voyages. In his *Observations Made During a Voyage Around the World* (1778), he wrote about their exploration of Tanna, where they stayed for two weeks. On 17 August 1774 Forster wrote: 'We came into a wood . . . where a dove of a new species was shot. It is a small dove, with both head and breast a rusty brown, but what marks it off from the other new doves is the dark green wings and the strangely yellow eyes.'[54] The entry continues with a detailed description of its 'black bill, red feet, grey belly and dark reddish-purple back'.[55] One of the surprises is Forster's discovery of the wild nutmeg, found in the crop of the Tanna Dove they had shot. They had been unable to locate the tree, but they now knew of its existence because of the bird. It is thought that the Tanna Dove was extinct by 1800.

Other pigeons and doves have existed in various parts of the world and gone unnoticed. How many are extinct without us having a record of them, or few details? Little is known of the Norfolk Island Pigeon (Columbidae *Hemiphaga novaeseelandiae spadicea*); the last recorded sighting of it was in 1801.[56] Another pigeon, the Lord Howe Island Pigeon (Columbidae *Columba vitiensis godmanae*), is known to us because of a painting made by Midshipman George Raper, who was aboard HMS *Sirius* in 1790 when the ship stopped at Lord Howe Island to stock up with supplies. It was not until 1915 that people realized that the painting was all they had of the bird; no specimens had ever been collected.[57] The birds' gentleness and fearlessness resulted in their destruction. They were easy to catch, and many were taken on European ships as a food source. In 1788 the surgeon Arthur Bowes of the *Lady Penrhyn*, wrote of the birds on Lord Howe Island: 'The Pidgeons were the largest I ever saw . . . the Pidgeons also were as tame as those already described and would sit upon the branches of the trees till you might go and take them off with your hands . . . many hundreds of all sorts . . . were caught and carried on board our ship with the *Charlotte*.'[58] By 1853 the Lord Howe Island Pigeon was extinct.

Pigeons have become extinct in many regions of the world. Between 1950 and 1985 the Mariana Fruit Dove and the White-throated Ground Dove disappeared from Guam. The reason for their extinction was the Brown Tree Snake (*Boiga irregularis*), thought to have arrived from Australia or New Guinea as stowaways on planes or ships. The dense forests, plentiful food and lack of predators meant that the snakes thrived. The only other snakes that have been on Guam had been the size of earthworms, so the bird population had no fear or experience of the invaders and no innate defences against them.

But there have been success stories as well. The Pink Pigeon, a threatened species found only on the island of Mauritius, was the subject of a breeding campaign by the late naturalist Gerald Durrell. Even while describing its beauty, overawed by

'Colombe à Moustaches', *Columba dominicensis*. Engraving by César Macret after Madame Knip, from *Les Pigeons* (Paris, 1811).

Colombe à Moustaches.
COLUMBA DOMINICENSIS *Lath*

contemplating this rare bird, Durrell slips into disparaging commentary concerning its intelligence and personality:

As we approached the wire, they peered at us in the mildly interested, oafish way that pigeons have and then, dismissing us from what passed for their minds, they fell into a doze. I felt that even though their rarity made them

of great biological and avicultural importance, one could hardly say that they had personalities that inspired one.[59]

Later, he writes: 'The female, like all female pigeons, succeeded in looking vacant, affronted and hysterical all at once, like a Regency maiden about to have the vapours.'[60] He continues in this vein: 'Given their tameness – or was it merely stupidity? – I was surprised that there were any of the species left.'[61]

Once Durrell captures the pigeon, his thoughts change a little:

Gazing at it, feeling its silken feathering against my fingers and sensing the steady tremor of its heart-beat and its breathing, I was filled with a great sadness. This was one of the thirty-three individuals that survived; the shipwrecked remnants of their species, eking out a precarious existence on their cryptomeria raft. So, at one time, must a tiny group of Dodos, the last of their harmless, waddling kind, have faced the final onslaught of

Dodo, coloured engraving after a detail from Roelandt Savery, *Fall of Adam*, 1626, formerly in the Königliche National-Galerie zu Berlin.

189

pigs, dogs, cats, monkeys and man, and disappeared for ever since there was no one to care and no one to offer them a breeding sanctuary, safe from their enemies.[62]

Durrell's Jersey Wildlife Preservation Trust (now the Durrell Wildlife Conservation Trust), has continued its captive breeding programme of the pink pigeon in Mauritius, the USA and Europe. Now the captive pink pigeon population numbers about 180 birds (in 1993 there were only 21 pink pigeons detected in the wild in Mauritius). As the pink pigeon is limited to the island of Mauritius, programmes such as these are a way to preserve an endangered species so that it doesn't suffer the same fate as its cousin the dodo.

In 2008 BirdLife International, in its list of globally threatened birds, officially declared the Liverpool Pigeon extinct. The Spotted Green Pigeon (*Caloenas maculata*), known as the Liverpool Pigeon because the only surviving specimen is held in World Museum Liverpool, was put on display after this announcement. BirdLife International only recognized this species in 2008 and then immediately declared it extinct. Its place of origin and the reasons for its extinction are unknown. It is thought to have been a forest dweller because of its green hue.

Of the large bird families in the world, few contain such a high proportion of endangered and threatened species. Most of these pigeons/doves live on islands. These areas need to bring in laws and regulations to control or prohibit shooting, establish protected areas, monitor the loss of habitat, establish captive populations for reintroduction back into the wild and then move more individual birds to new, suitable areas to increase the bird population.

Casting aside the almost storybook tales about the dodo, and the hard to imagine numbers of the now extinct passenger pigeons, the cold facts are that of 318 species of columbid, 13 are already extinct, and around 59 species of pigeons and doves are threatened with extinction (approximately 20 per cent of all species). Do we need to put aside our prejudices in order to preserve and protect the pigeon?

Zhang Huan, *Seeds of Hamburg*, performance, Hamburg, Kunstuerein, 2002.

Conclusion

The pigeon. If we cannot appreciate its beauty, perhaps we can admire its navigational skills, its ability to adapt, or its part in changing the course of human history – from its role in the development of evolutionary theory to influencing the outcome of wars.

In Bob Graham's book *How To Heal A Broken Wing* (2008), a young child notices an injured pigeon; the adults do not. Maybe we have to learn to 'see' through the innocence and excitement of a child's eye, or through the heart of an artist. In Omega Goodwin's *Pigeons of Melbourne* project (2007) pink fibreglass lifesized pigeons congregate in public spaces, alongside humans. They are part of our landscape, and remind us that we too are communal. On 13 June 2008 New York City celebrated National Pigeon Day, a day 'in defense of the city pigeon', as well as an event celebrating their history which is interwoven with our own. This date was chosen to coincide with the death of Cher Ami, the pigeon credited with saving the lives of 194 US infantrymen in France during World War I (see pp. 114–5), on 13 June 1919.

Perhaps we have distanced ourselves from our feathered companions. We have become too sophisticated to enjoy the little creature who resides alongside us in the cities, who shares our space. Do we need to 'name' our *columba livia*, to permit a bond to be formed, or, if not a bond, then at least an acknowledgement of the pigeons' part in the drama of history, religion and culture? In the past they have been involved in the war effort, facing gunfire and other dangers, as they endeavoured to deliver the messages entrusted to them. In peacetime we need to protect them from enemy fire and destruction, and learn how to cohabit in these cities of concrete cliffs and steel ledges. Dove or pigeon? Light or shadow? Dove of peace or rat with wings? The terms we use define and judge us, rather than the magnificent, yet humble, rock pigeon.

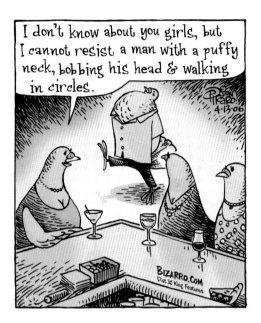

Cartoon by Dan Piraro (Bizarro). Pigeons have fascinated people for centuries, and there is no reason to suppose that this will cease. While sometimes objects of fun, they continue to be objects of admiration.

Timeline of the Pigeon

140 MYA	MIOCENE EPOCH	3,000 BCE

Archaeopteryx ('ancient wing').

(10–20 million years ago): columbiformes evolved.

Domesticated in Egypt.
Set aside for sacrifice in the Old Testament.

1681	1815	1870–71	1896

Dodo (*Raphus cucullatus*) extinct.

Earliest pigeon race in Europe held in Belgium.

Siege of Paris, messages delivered by pigeons.

First organized pigeon airmail service.

1969	2000	2007

PBS children's series, 'Sesame Street' begins, with a cast member, Bert, who loves pigeons, and invents a dance called 'Doing the Pigeon'.

London's Mayor, Ken Livingstone, declares war on the pigeons of Trafalgar Square.

Feeding pigeons in Trafalgar Square is outlawed.

6th century BCE	30	1574	1592
Pigeon post set up by Cyrus the Great, covering regions of Ancient near East.	Baptism of Jesus: Holy Spirit portrayed as a dove.	War of Independence in Holland: during the 6-month siege of Leyden, citizens saved by pigeons delivering messages.	Constellation *Columba* named by Dutch astronomer and cartographer Petrus Plancius.

1900	1 September 1914	WORLD WAR 1	1943
Last documented wild passenger pigeon shot in Ohio, 24 March.	Death of the last passenger pigeon, Martha, in the Cincinnati Zoo.	100,000 pigeons used in the war effort.	Introduction of the Dickin Medal, for heroic animals who were part of the war service. The first recipient of the medal was a pigeon, Winkie.

2007	2008	13 JUNE 2008
British Parliament bans pigeon racing from the mainland of continental Europe to Britain, because of the perceived risk of avian flu.	The Spotted Green Pigeon (*caloenas maculata*: known as the Liverpool Pigeon) declared extinct.	National Pigeon Day, New York.

United Nations General Assembly

References

INTRODUCTION

1 Carl A. Naether, *The Book of the Pigeon and of Wild Foreign Doves* (New York, 1964), p. v.
2 Ibid.
3 There are, of course, exceptions to this disdain for the pigeon in public places. At Walt Disney World Resort in Orlando, Florida, a loft for pigeons has been constructed. Every day hundreds of pigeons are released to be part of the activities of the theme park.
4 R. Wright Campbell, *Where Pigeons Go to Die* (Sarasota, FL, 1978), p. 1.
5 M. Proust, *Remembrance of Things Past*, vol. I, *Swann's Way* (London, 1982), p. 442.

1 PIGEON OR DOVE?

1 In Sanskrit there are thirty different words for 'pigeon'.
2 Charles Darwin, *The Illustrated Origin of Species*, abridged and introduced by Robert E. Leakey (London, 1979), p. 17.
3 Peter Hansell and Jean Hansell, *Doves and Dovecotes* (Bath, 1988), p. 9.
4 Ibid, p. 11.
5 Ibid.
6 Ibid.
7 Ibid.
8 Virginia C. Holmgren, *Bird Walk through the Bible* (New York,

1972), p. 89.

9   Hansell and Hansell, *Doves and Dovecotes*, p. 11.

10 Holmgren, *Bird Walk through the Bible*, p. 89: 'The time of the singing of birds is come, and the voice of the turtle is heard in our land.'

11 Darwin, *The Illustrated Origin of Species*, p. 55.

12 Writers vary on numbers of species that belong in the family Columbidae. How to classify them? At the first International Congress of Zoologists, held in Paris in 1889, a system of classifying, devised a century earlier by Carl Linnaeus, was implemented. The Linnaean system consists of using a two-word Latin label for each individual kind. This was called a *species*. The next step of classification was called the *class*. *Class* was divided into groups called *Orders*, then each *order* into subdivisions called *Genera* (or 'kind'). Each member of a *Genera* was called a *Species*, which meant that there was no bird (animal, plant) like it. Later, scientists inserted another step, which served to subdivide each *Order* into *Families*, and each *Family* into *Genera* and *Species*. When we consider the rock pigeon, we would say it is in the *Class: Aves* (Latin for 'bird'), *Order:* Columbiformes, *Family:* Columbidae, *Genus: Columba* and *Species:* . . . The *family* Columbidae is usually divided into five *sub-families*: for the rock dove or rock pigeon, it is *Columba livia*. The two-word Latin label for official use is made up of the name of the genus (written first and capitalized) and the name of the species (for example *Columba livia*). Holmgren, *Bird Walk through the Bible*, pp. 21–2.

13 From the National Geographic television series 'Brilliant Beasts' (2007). The photography, showing the pigeons taking off, is breathtaking.

14 Accessed at www.uscg.mil/history/articles/pigeonsSARProject.asp; www.susanscott.net/OceanWatch2001/jun22-01.html.

15 This theory was demonstrated by research from Ruhr University Bochum, Germany. A pigeon was placed in a Skinner box (named after B. F. Skinner, who pioneered work for the US Army as part of Project Pigeon, which was later dropped in order to pursue

electronic methods). In the box there were plastic pecking keys on the walls. The pigeon was to peck the keys that were in line with the direction of polarized light (which was altered during other tests). The pigeon would be rewarded if it pecked at the key. This demonstrated that pigeons have sensitivity to the polarization of light. This polarization is strong in the wavelengths of ultraviolet rays. Pigeons were tested, again using the Skinner box, to see if they would peck whenever they saw a light flash. Different frequencies were used, including the shorter wavelength of ultraviolet light; the pigeons responded to both 'visible' and 'invisible' light.

16 William Shakespeare, *Hamlet*, Act 2, Scene 2.
17 Some are adamant that this method is unique to pigeons, others suggest there are one or two other birds that drink in a similar fashion.
18 Gilbert White, *The Illustrated Natural History of Selborne* [1789] (London, 1981), p. 95.
19 D. Goodwin, 'Behaviour', in *Physiology and Behaviour of the Pigeon*, ed. Michael Abs (London, 1983), p. 287.
20 T. H. White, *The Sword in the Stone* [1938] (London, 1976), p. 210.
21 Adele Nozedar, *The Secret Language of Birds: A Treasury of Myths, Folklore and Inspirational True Stories* (London, 2006), p. 241.
22 Michael M. Vriends and Tommy E. Erskine, *Pigeons*, 2nd edn (Hauppauge, NY, 2005), p. 53.
23 Edward Lear, *Later Letters of Edward Lear*, ed. Lady Strachy (London, 1911), pp. 354–5.
24 Shakespeare, *Hamlet*, speech of Gertrude, Queen of Denmark, Act 5, Scene 1.
25 E. B. White, *The Points of My Compass* (London, 1963), p. 104.
26 William Shakespeare, *As You Like It*, Act 1, Scene 2.
27 Darwin, *The Illustrated Origin of Species*.
28 Ibid, p. 53.
29 Ian Kilgower and Robert Kilgower, *Australian Racing Pigeons* (Adelaide, 1982), pp. 55–60. This section on feather pigments owes a lot to the Kilgowers' summary, as well as to Wendell Mitchell Levi, *The Pigeon* (Columbia, SC, 1941).

30 Ibid, p. 55.
31 Kevin Cleasby, *Pigeon Genetics for Beginners* (Victoria Park, Western Australia, 1999), p. 36.
32 Cited in Robert Fulton, *The Illustrated Book of Pigeons with Standards for Judging* (London, 1874–6; *Pigeon Classics*, vol. III of *Fulton & Lumley's Illustrated Book of Pigeons*, rewritten and edited by K. Cleasby (Perth, 2001), p. 11.
33 Jonathan Balcombe, *Pleasurable Kingdom* (Basingstoke, 2006), p. 52.
34 Ibid.
35 One example in regard to the intelligence of pigeons is an experiment, the results of which were published in 1982, whereby B. F. Skinner and colleagues of Harvard University trained pigeons to locate coloured spots placed on their chests and peck at them. Once the pigeons had mastered this, bibs were placed on them, and the dot could only be seen in a mirror. When the pigeons noticed the dot reflected in the mirror, they did not peck at the mirror, instead they pecked at the dots under their bibs. Rather than accord the pigeons with high intelligence, the researchers concluded that 'if a bird can do it, it cannot be complex behaviour and it cannot indicate self-awareness of any sort.' Balcombe, *Pleasurable Kingdom*, pp. 51–2.
36 Nozedar, *The Secret Language of Birds*, p. 31.
37 R. J. Herrnstein and D. H. Loveland, 'Complex Visual Concept in the Pigeon', *Science*, 146 (1964), pp. 549–51.
38 Donald S. Blough, 'Pigeon Perception of Letters of the Alphabet', *Science*, 218 (1982), pp. 397–8.
39 Ibid., p. 397.
40 *Telegraph.co.uk*, 13 June 2008.
41 S. Watanabe, J. Sakamoto and M. Wakita, 'Pigeons' Discrimination of Paintings by Monet and Picasso', *Journal of the Experimental Analysis of Behavior*, LXIII/2 (1995), pp. 165–74.
42 For a complete list of the paintings used in the experiments see ibid., pp. 167–8, available at www.pubmedcentral.nih.gov/picrender.fcgi?artid=133439&blobtype=pdf.

43 Ibid., p. 173.

44 Ibid., p. 165.

45 D. Porter and A. Neuringer, 'Musical Discrimination by Pigeons',
    Journal of Experimental Psychology: Animal Behavior Processes, 10
    (1984), pp. 138–48.

46 Stravinsky's *Firebird Suite* for orchestra; a Buxtehude organ work;
    a Vivaldi concerto for violin and orchestra; Elliott Carter's Sonata
    for Flute, Oboe, Cello and Harpsichord; Walter Piston's *Chromatic
    Study on the Name of Bach* for organ and a Scarlatti harpsichord
    sonata.

47 Ibid; p. 138. It is worth noting opposing viewpoints in the scientific
    world: those, following on from the work of Lloyd-Morgan (1894),
    who caution against attributing anthropomorphic descriptions of
    complex animal behaviours, and the alternative school of thought
    (which includes Aristotle, Romanes, Lorenz and contemporary sci-
    entists involved in animal behaviour and ethology, such as Marc
    Berkoff), who maintain that animals are similar to humans, or,
    going to the next step, stating that if we recognize we are all ani-
    mals, we will of course display similarities as well as differences.

48 Boria Sax, *The Parliament of Animals: Anecdotes and Legends from
    Books of Natural History 1775–1900* (New York, 1992), p. 168. 'I
    observed that pigeons seem to be attracted to music when we re-
    homed several fancy pigeons. I would play music for an hour each
    evening, as they settled for the evening in their cages, having been
    free all day. The music seemed to be a great attraction; the pigeons
    would move to the front of the cages to listen to the radio, and coo
    away to different pieces of music (seeming to have a preference for
    classical and opera). Previously, we had been nursing an injured
    squab. While he was recovering he would come into the house
    each evening to listen to the radio. Perched on the back of a kitchen
    chair, he would dance and coo, becoming quite agitated when we
    would turn off the radio to settle him for the night. Even when he
    was well enough to fly away, he would come back each morning for
    a feed, and each evening he would sit outside the back door, to lis-
    ten to the music before flying off to roost for the night. Jazz seemed

to be his music of choice.'

49 Clive D. L. Wynne, *Do Animals Think?* (Princeton, NJ, and Oxford, 2004), p. 147.

50 Klaus Schmidt-Koenig in *Physiology and Behaviour of the Pigeon*, ed. Michael Abs, p. 268.

51 Ibid, p. 273.

52 Ibid., p. 280.

53 Balcombe, *Pleasurable Kingdom*, p. 53.

54 Ibid., p. 53. The researchers were from Oxford University.

55 Jon Carroll, 'With No Direction Home', *San Francisco Chronicle*, 11 January 1996, cited in Larry Harbegger and Amy G. Carlson, *The Gift of Birds* (San Francisco, CA, 1999), p. 294.

56 Ibid., p. 295.

2 HEAVEN-SENT: RELIGION AND MYTHOLOGY

1 'The Dove's Nature and Allegory' (*c.* 13th century), in *A Medieval Bestiary*, trans. T. J. Elliot (Boston, MA, 1971), pp. 35–6.

2 Joseph Campbell, *The Masks of God: Primitive Mythology* (Harmondsworth, 1969), p. 368.

3 Miriam Rothschild, *Butterfly Cooing like A Dove* (London, 1991), p. 21. Other sources do not portray Eurynome in this way, but instead list her as one of Zeus' wives.

4 Jan Knappert, *An Encyclopedia of Myth and Legend: African Mythology* (London, 1995), p. 74.

5 Aboriginal (or indigenous Australian) Dreamtime is the part of aboriginal culture that explains the origins of the universe and how and why humans were created. It deals with spirituality and beliefs, of 'time before time' or 'the time of creation'.

6 Hugh Rule and Stuart Goodman, *Gulpilil's Stories of the Dreamtime* (Sydney, 1979), pp. 107–16. Another legend from the Aboriginal Dreamtime tells of the destiny of the wonga pigeon, which was attacked by a hawk and falls into a clump of white waratah flowers, turning them red with its blood. This is the reason for the crimson colour of the waratah flowers.

7 R. Campbell Thompson, *The Devils and Evil Spirits of Babylonia*, vol. II (London, 1903–14), 14.2.76; trans. corrected by D. Wright, cited in Jacob Milgrom, *Leviticus 1–16: A New Translation with Introduction and Commentary* (New York, 1991), p. 834.

8 Peter Hansell and Jean Hansell, *Doves and Dovecotes* (Bath, 1988), p. 16.

9 Ibid.

10 Rothschild, *Butterfly Cooing like a Dove*, p. 108.

11 George Cansdale, *Animals of Bible Lands* (Exeter, 1970), p. 136.

12 Wendell Mitchell Levi, *The Pigeon* (Columbia, SC, 1941), p. 2.

13 Tibullus (54–19 BC), *Eighth Elegy*, quoted by Lyell (1897) and cited in ibid.

14 Ibid, p. 213.

15 Ibid, p. 161. Another version is that the Pleiades were the daughters of the Titan Atlas and the sea-nymph Pleione. One day when Pleoine and her daughters were playing outside, Orion the hunter saw them and was struck by their beauty. He began to pursue them. Zeus, noticing their plight, changed Pleione and her daughters into doves to escape Orion. Zeus then turned them into a small group of stars.

16 Adele Nozedar, *The Secret Language of Birds: A Treasury of Myths, Folklore and Inspirational True Stories* (London, 2006), p. 242.

17 *Brewer's Dictionary of Phrase & Fable*, revd Adrian Room (London, 2001), p. 352, 136. One of the Sirens is said to have followed a message from a dove to find a place to set up a city. This city became Naples (Nozedar, *The Secret Language of Birds*, p. 243).

18 Virginia C. Holmgren, *Birds of the Bible* (New York, 1972), p. 34.

19 Walter Ferguson, *Living Animals of the Bible* (New York, 1974)

20 Roy Pinney, *Animals in the Bible* (Philadelphia, PA, 1964), p. 161.

21 *Brewer's Dictionary of Phrase and Fable*, Millennium edn, revd Adrian Room (London, 2001), p. 477. The story goes that pigeons have no gall because the dove that was sent from the ark by Noah burst its gall in grief: and none of the pigeon family has had a gall ever since.

22 Stefan Zweig, 'Legend of the Third Dove', in *Gates to the New City:*

A Treasury of Modern Jewish Tales, ed. Howard Schwartz (New York, 1983).

23 In Ann and Reg Cartwright's *Norah's Ark* (Harmondsworth, 1983), there is a magpie and an owl, but no dove.

24 Allan's *The Dove* (London, 2004) was originally published as *The Bird* (1997).

25 Rothschild, *Butterfly Cooing like a Dove*, p. 136.

26 John Gardner Wilkinson, *Manners and Customs of the Ancient Egyptians*, 1 (London, 1837), p. 301. In Oscar Wilde's 'The Nightingale and the Rose', the rose bush exclaims that '"My roses are red," it answered, "as red as the feet of the dove."' Another legend among the Rengma Nagas of Nagaland, India, deals with the colour of the dove's feet. A green magpie hears God telling the dove that if he arrives early in the morning, God will paint his legs bright red. The next day the green magpie wakes up very early, and rushes to God, arriving before the dove, so the green magpie's legs receives a brilliant red for its colour. When the dove finally arrives, the only colour left is dull red. Rothschild, *Butterfly Cooing like a Dove*, p. 114.

27 *The Epic of Gilgamesh*, ed. and trans. Benjamin R. Foster (New York, 2001), pp. 88–9.

28 Then Enkidu descends to the 'house of shadows',

> To the house whose dwellers are deprived of light,
> Where dust is their fare and their food is clay.
> They are dressed like birds in feather garments.

Ibid., p. 58.

29 Nozedar, *The Secret Language of Birds*, p. 188.

30 Cansdale, *Animals of Bible Lands*, p. 170.

31 Levi, *The Pigeon*, p. 2.

32 Bernard Lazare, *Le Fumier de Job* (Paris, 1928), cited in Rothschild, *Butterfly Cooing like a Dove*, p. 156.

33 A commentary from the *Midrash*:

King Agrippa wished to offer up a thousand burnt offerings in one day. He sent to tell the high priest, 'let no man other than myself offer sacrifices today!' There came a poor man with two turtledoves in his hand, and he said to the high priest, 'Sacrifice these.' Said he: 'The king commanded me, saying, "Let no man other than myself offer sacrifices this day."' Said he: 'My Lord the high priest, I catch four [doves] every day: two I offer up. And with the other two I sustain myself. If you do not offer them up, you cut off my means of sustenance.' The priest took them and offered them up. In a dream it was revealed to Agrippa: 'The sacrifice of a poor man preceded yours.' So he went to the high priest saying: 'Did I not command you thus: "Let no one but me offer sacrifices this day?"' Said [the high priest] to him: 'Your Majesty, a poor man came with two turtledoves in his hand, and said to me: "I catch four birds every day; I sacrifice two, and from the other two I support myself. If you will not offer them up you will cut off my means of sustenance." Should I not have offered them up?' Said [King Agrippa] to him: 'You were right in doing as you did.'

(*Midrash Lev. Rab.* 3:5). Milgrom, *Leviticus 1–16*, pp. 166–7.

34 Holmgren, *Birds of the Bible*, p. 87: '"Stool" was the English name for the little open cage that kept the decoy in place.' 'Like a decoy partridge in a cage' (Sirach 11:30–31).

35 Ibid. Holmgren suggests that the word 'pet' may have its origins in the Greek word *peteinon*, the word for small bird, or birds in general.

36 F. S. Bodenheimer, *Animal and Man in Bible Lands* (Leiden, 1960), p. 23. There are drawings of birds, including a rock dove and a turtledove, in the Temple of Tuthmosis III at Karnak.

37 Oded Borowski, *Every Living Thing: Daily Use of Animals in Ancient Israel* (London, 1998), p. 158.

38 Ibid.

39 Ibid.

40 Ibid.

41 Ibid.

42 The writer continues, describing his lover as a dove: 'O my dove, in the clefts of the rock, in the covert of the cliff' (Song of Solomon, 2:14). Other Biblical references to doves include Isaiah 38:14 and Ezekiel 7:16.

43 'Leave the towns, and live on the rock, O inhabitants of Moab! Be like the dove that nests on the sides of the mouth of a gorge' (Jeremiah 43:28) is a reference to the rock pigeons' tendency to nest on steep rock faces is a barb directed at the inhabitants of Moab. 'Do not deliver the soul of your dove to the wild animals; do not forget the life of your poor forever' (Psalms 74:19), an injunction to remember the poor, is poignant in its comparison of the poor to the innocent doves. The next verses mention the need to uphold the covenant, which included caring for the poor.

44 Holmgren, *Birds of the Bible*, p. 93.

45 Ibid.

46 *Mishnah*, Sanhedrin 111:3.

47 Levi, *The Pigeon*, p. 4.

48 In John Watters, *Birds of Ireland* (Dublin, 1853), cited in Walter Harter, *Birds in Fact and Legend* (New York, 1979), p. 33.

49 There is a reference to doves being present at the birth of Jesus in the apocryphal *Gospel of the Holy Twelve*: 'And there were in the same cave an ox and a horse and an ass and a sheep, and beneath the manger was a cat with her little ones; and there were doves also overhead; and each had its mate after its kind, the male with the female.'

50 Holmgren, *Birds of the Bible*, p. 169.

51 Other accounts depict the dove bringing the wafer to the Holy Grail. Some mention that the attendants in charge of the Grail wore white cloaks embroidered with golden doves.

52 Another source gives her name as Quendreda: David Farmer, in *The Oxford Dictionary of Saints* (Oxford, 1987), p. 249.

53 Jennifer Westwood and Jacqueline Simpson, *The Lore of the Land: A Guide to England's Legends, from Spring-Heeled Jack to the Witches of Warboys* (London, 2005), p. 806.

54 Doves are not always the bird of choice; the Venerable Bede is associated with the woodpigeon.

55 Paul Sabatier, *The Road to Assisi: The Essential Biography of St Francis*, ed. Jon M. Sweeney (Brewster, MA, 2003), p. 166, cited in Debra K. Farrington, *All God's Creatures: The Blessing of Animal Companions* (Brewster, MA, 2006) pp. 52–3. Another tale is that of St Tathan, who had two tame doves that would wander around the refectory. One day, one of the doves was captured by a kite. Tathan was upset when told of the capture, but prayed that God would restore the dove to him. The following day, after the celebration of Mass, the kite flew down, holding the dove in his claws. He placed the dove, safe and sound, at the feet of Tathan. Tathan exclaimed: 'Here is the dove which was dead: she is now alive again . . . I praise the Creator: such comfort he bestows upon his servant.' David N. Bell, *Wholly Animals: A Book of Beastly Tales* (Kalamazoo, MI, 1992), p. 118.

56 Hugh of St Victor, *De bestris et allis rebus*, Book 1, cited in Rothschild, *Butterfly Cooing like a Dove*, p. 114.

57 William Shakespeare, *Henry IV, Part II*, Act IV, Scene 1.

58 Hansell and Hansell, *Doves and Dovecotes*, p. 16.

59 Ibid.

60 Walter Harter, *Feathered Heroes: Pigeons from Ancient Times to Now* (New York, 1968), pp. 34–5.

61 Michael J. Curley, trans., *Physiologus* (Austin, TX, and London, 1979), p. 57.

62 Ibid., pp. 64–6, and Ron Baxter, *Bestiaries and their Users in the Middle Ages* (Phoenix Mill, 1998), p. 54.

63 Bell, *Wholly Animals*, p. 10.

64 In Japanese *yama-bato* means 'mountain pigeon'.

65 Nozedar, *The Secret Language of Birds*, p. 169.

66 Dhan Gopal Mukerji, *Gay-Neck: The Story of a Pigeon* [1928] (London, 1938), p. 1.

67 Nozedar, *The Secret Language of Birds*, p. 245.

68 Ibid., p. 204.

69 Ibid., p. 243.

70 Campbell, *The Masks of God*, p. 294.

71 Nozedar, *The Secret Language of Birds*, p. 246.

72 Rothschild, *Butterfly Cooing like a Dove*, p. 107.

73 Mark Haeffner, *Dictionary of Alchemy* (London, 1994), p. 42.

74 Westwood and Simpson, *The Lore of the Land*, pp. 616–17.

75 *South Wales Echo*, 15 July 1902, cited in Nozedar, *The Secret Language of Birds*, p. 244.

76 Ibid., p. 146.

77 Westwood and Simpson, *The Lore of the Land*, p. 245.

78 Ibid.

79 From 'The Butcher's Boy', a traditional Anglo-American folk song.

80 Nozedar, *The Secret Language of Birds*, p. 474.

3 AN UNEASY RELATIONSHIP: MEDICINE, MEAT AND MESSENGERS

1 Peter Hansell and Jean Hansell, *Doves and Dovecotes* (Bath, 1998), p. 28.

2 Ibid.

3 Ibid.

4 Ibid.

5 Samuel Pepys, *The Diary of Samuel Pepys*, vol. IV, ed. Robert Latham and William Matthews (London, 1971), p. 339.

6 Hansell and Hansell, *Doves and Dovecotes*.

7 Ibid.

8 Jonathan Balcombe, *Pleasurable Kingdom: Animals and the Nature of Feeling Good* (Basingstoke, 2006), p. 163.

9 Jack Kligerman, *A Fancy for Pigeons* (New York, 1978), p. 98.

10 Ibid. Freedom Fields Hospital has since closed.

11 Walter Harter, *Feathered Heroes: Pigeons from Ancient Times to Now* (New York, 1968), p. 69.

12 The pigeon had been kept as a pet by one of the prisoners. 'The incident had prompted the prison administration to consider closing down a prisoner pigeon-breeding project established in a ward of the jail as part of a rehabilitation program' (*The Australian*, 23 August 2008). Another incident, involving pigeons being used by prisoners to deliver drugs and mobile phones, was uncovered in Brazil earlier in 2008.

13 Hansell and Hansell, *Doves and Dovecotes*, p. 23.

14 Wendell M. Levi, *Making Pigeons Pay* (New York, 1946), p. 2.

15 Hansell and Hansell, *Doves and Dovecotes*, p. 40.

16 Ibid. *Testudo* is Latin for tortoise. Here it means 'an arched roof'.

17 Ibid., p. 41.

18 Hansell and Hansell, *Doves and Dovecotes*, p. 39.

19 John Seldon, *Table-talk* (London, 1689), cited in Kligerman, *A Fancy for Pigeons*, p. 67.

20 Ibid., p. 84. In 1651 it was estimated that England had 26,000 dovecotes.

21 Hansell and Hansell, *Doves and Dovecotes*, p. 78.

22 Cited in Kligerman, *A Fancy for Pigeons*, p. 84.

23 Ibid.

24 Ibid., p. 85.

25 From Thomas Tusser, 1580, cited in Hansell and Hansell, *Doves and Dovecotes*, p. 55.

26 Hansell and Hansell, *Doves and Dovecotes*, p. 56.

27 Ibid., p. 56.

28 Ibid., p. 46.

29 Ibid., p. 58.

30 Ibid., p. 58.

31 Ibid.

32 Virginia C. Holmgren, *Bird Walk through the Bible* (New York), 1975, p. 92.

33 Levi, *Making Pigeons Pay*, p. 3.

34 Ibid., p. 5.

35 Kligerman, *A Fancy for Pigeons*, p. 87.

36 From John Moore, *Columbarium*, cited in ibid. Moore was correct in this regard, for pigeon dung is an excellent source of potassium nitrate.

37 Hansell and Hansell, *Doves and Dovecotes*, p. 30.

38 Ibid.

39 At http://jewelry-blog.internetstones.com/famous-gemstones/ nga-mark-kallahpyan-rubies.

40 Richard W. Hughes, 'Pigeon's Blood: A Pilgrimage to Mogok – Valley of Rubies', available at http://ruby-sapphire.com/pigeons-

blood-mogok.htm (accessed 26 May 2009).

41 James B. Nelson, *Journal of Gemmology*, xix (1985), p. 7, cited in
    ibid. In a longer version of the quote, Nelson said that the pigeon
    blood 'was indeed the match to the colour of these unique rubies'
    (cited at www.gubelinlab.com/TradeColours/.asp. This is inter-
    esting, because the conclusion of the quote cited in Hughes would
    lead one to presume that the ruby was *not* the colour of pigeon
    blood. As an aside, in Burma, the second best colour to class
    rubies is termed 'rabbits' blood'; it is slightly darker than pigeon
    blood, with a bluish tinge.

42 Diane Morgan, *Fire and Blood: Rubies in Myth, Magic and History*
    (Westport, CT, 2007), p. 36.

43 Hansell and Hansell, *Doves and Dovecotes*, p. 17.

44 Frontinus, *Stratagems*, III: xiii: 8.

45 Hansell and Hansell, *Doves and Dovecotes*, pp. 17–18.

46 Walter Harter, *Feathered Heroes: Pigeons from Ancient Times to Now*
    (New York, 1968), p. 21.

47 Cited in ibid., pp. 22–3.

48 Hansell and Hansell, *Doves and Dovecotes*, p. 19.

49 Ibid., p. 23.

50 Hansell and Hansell, *Doves and Dovecotes*, p. 17.

51 Stephen Green-Armytage, *Extraordinary Pigeons* (New York,
    2003), p. 99.

52 Hansell and Hansell, *Doves and Dovecotes*, p. 19.

53 Harter, *Feathered Heroes*, p. 75.

54 Green-Armytage, *Extraordinary Pigeons*, p. 99.

55 Wendell Mitchell Levi, *The Pigeon* (Columbia, SC, 1941), p. 10.

56 Hansell and Hansell, *Doves and Dovecotes*, p. 19.

57 Levi, *The Pigeon*, p. 5.

58 Clive D. L. Wynne, *Do Animals Think?* (Princeton and Oxford,
    2004), p. 151.

59 Hansell and Hansell, *Doves and Dovecotes*, p. 20.

60 Levi, *The Pigeon*, p. 7. Between 9,000 and 10,000 pigeons were
    British war homers.

61 Juliet Gardiner, *The Animals' War* (London, 2006), p. 100.

62 Ibid.

63 Ibid.

64 Ibid., p. 102.

65 Levi, *The Pigeon*, p. 7.

66 Hansell and Hansell, *Doves and Dovecotes*, p. 22.

67 Cited in Wynne, *Do Animals Think?*, p. 140. Cher Ami is on display in the Smithsonian Institute in Washington, DC. There were many other brave pigeons, including President Wilson, the Mocker and Big Tom, John Silver, Colonel's Lady, Spike, Lord Adelaide and the Poilu.

68 Miriam Rothschild, *Butterfly Cooing like a Dove* (London, 1991), p. 108.

69 Gardiner, *The Animals' War*, p. 102.

70 Hitler wasn't a vegetarian; the myth of Hitler's vegetarianism was carefully formulated by Nazi Germany's minister of propaganda, Joseph Goebbels. In Nazi Germany, vegetarian societies were banned; see Charles Patterson, *Eternal Treblinka* (New York, 2002), pp. 126–8.

71 The childrens' book *Lofty's Mission* addresses the use of homing pigeons for the war effort in World War II, and the citizens who were willing to donate their best pigeons to the cause.

72 Kapoor Priya and Jaishankar Nandita, *Very Important Pets* (London, 2004), p. 65.

73 Ibid., p. 67.

74 Anthony Hill, *Animal Heroes* (London, 2005), p. 214.

75 Ibid., pp. 214–15.

76 As in the numbering of inmates in concentration camps; to make them less than they were. With the pigeons, perhaps it was to remind the troops that the pigeons were there to perform a task; to lessen the chance of forming a bond.

77 Hansell and Hansell, *Doves and Dovecotes*, p. 36.

78 The other survivor was the Prince of Rome, owned by a man from Bishop Auckland, Co. Durham.

79 Sudbury has written a children's book about the story of the King of Rome, *King of Rome* (Vancouver, 2008). See www.derbypictures.

co.uk/features/kingofrome/index.htm for additional information, including a YouTube clip of the song, with photographs of the King of Rome and a race map.

80 Carl A. Naether, *The Book of the Pigeon and of Wild Foreign Doves* (New York, 1964), p. 13.
81 *Guardian*, available at http://guardian.co.uk/uk/2008/jan/21/ birdflu.uknews4, 21 January 2008.
82 Jock Grey, pigeon racer, cited in *Vegan Voice*, 34 (June–August 2008), p. 14. Although this is Grey's perception of the bond, this is a generalization. Some pigeon racers kill, sell off or give away pigeons that can no longer fly long distances in record time, breed, or have a good chance of winning a race.
83 Cited in a review of Michael Boulter's *Darwin's Garden* (London, 2008) in *The Independent*, 9 July 2008, www.independent.co.uk/ news/science/origin-of-the-thesis-at-the-bottom-of-darwins-garden-862876.html.
84 *Daily Telegraph*, 27 November 2007.

4 LOVED OR LOATHED: PORTRAYALS IN LITERATURE, ART AND CULTURE

1 Wendell Mitchell Levi, *The Pigeon* (Columbia, SC, 1941), p. 10.
2 Ibid.
3 Ibid, p. 11.
4 See chapter Two for more examples.
5 Charles Dickens, *Barnaby Rudge: A Tale of the Riots of 'Eighty* (London, 1841), chap. 1.
6 E. B. White, *The Points of My Compass* (London, 1963), p. 103.
7 From Robert Browning, 'Two in the Campagna', in *The Poems*, vol. I, ed. John Pettigrew, supplemented and completed by Thomas J. Collins (London, 1981), p. 729.
8 Other films and productions which feature pigeons/doves include the black comedy cartoon series *King of the Hill*. One episode deals with pigeon extermination, and the love interest of the pigeon exterminator. By the end of the episode, the pigeons are

either exterminated, or spaced out by chemicals. The animated film *Shrek 2* has several scenes with pigeons and doves. Near the beginning of the film, when Fiona and Shrek arrive at the land of Far Far Away, doves are flying around the castle. When one spots Shrek, it flies off in fright, dives into the wall and falls dead at the feet of the king. In the Fairy Godmother's factory, when the cauldron filled with potion tips over, everyone turns into doves and pigeons. The long-running television series *Touched by an Angel* always has a white dove appear at the beginning of each episode, as the angels enter the lives of certain people. At the close of the episode the dove flies away, back to heaven.

9 John Milton, *Paradise Lost,* Book i, 17–23, in *Poetical Works*, ed. Douglas Bush (London, 1966), p. 212.

10 William Blake, from *Auguries of Innocence*, in *Blake: The Complete Poems*, ed. W. H. Stevenson, 3rd edn (Harlow, 2007), p. 612.

11 John Keats, *Complete Poems and Selected Letters*, intro. by Edward Hirsch (New York, 2001), p. 339.

12 Helen Ward, *The Animals' Christmas Carol* (Rowville, 2006).

13 Józef Wilkoń, *Thomas and the Dove* (Tunbridge Wells, 1989).

14 At www.cresourcei.org/cy/cy12days.html.

15 I am grateful to Andrew D. Blechman's book *Pigeons* (New York, 2006) for drawing my attention to this fact.

16 Chris d'Lacey, *Fly, Cherokee, Fly* (London, 1998), p. 8.

17 Isaac Bashevis Singer, 'Pigeons', from *A Friend of Kafka and Other Stories* (London, 1972), p. 124.

18 Abba Kovner, 'My little sister' in *My Little Sister*, trans. Shirley Kaufman (London, 1971).

19 Bohumil Hrabel, *I Served the King of England*, trans. Paul Wilson (London, 2006), pp. 196–7; 'and the rustling of feathers and wings was like flour or salt being poured out of a bag. The pigeons . . . would sit on my shoulders and fly around my head and beat their wings against my ears, blotting out the world, as though I were tangled up in a huge bridal train stretching in front of me and behind me, a veil of moving wings and eight hundred beautiful blueberry eyes . . . [I] ran across the yard with pigeons swirling around me

and swarming over me, because for them I was a god of life. And I looked back on my life and saw myself now, surrounded by these divine messengers, these pigeons, as though I were a saint.' This passage inspired artwork on display in the Brisbane Art Gallery.

20 *Aesop's Fables*, trans. Laura Gibbs (Oxford, 2002), p. 25.

21 John Donne, *The Complete English Poems*, ed. A. J. Smith (London, 1971), p. 47.

22 T. H. White, *The Sword in the Stone* [1938] (London, 1976), pp. 212–13.

23 Pam Ayres, *Bertha and the Racing Pigeon* (London, 1979), p. 7. The story follows the friendship between Bertha, a wood pigeon, and Fleet, a Red-Chequered Racing Homer.

24 Carlo Collodi, *Pinocchio* (New York, 2005), p. 70.

25 Ibid., p. 72. In Hans Christian Andersen's *The Snow Queen* two wood pigeons help Gerda on the next part of her journey.

26 Mo Willems, *The Pigeon Wants A Puppy!* (London, 2008). Other books in the series include *Don't Let the Pigeon Drive the Bus!, The Pigeon Finds a Hot Dog!* and *Don't Let the Pigeon Stay Up Late!*

27 R. Campbell Wright, *Where Pigeons Go to Die* (Sarasota, FL, 1978), p. 68.

28 In the film, Ghost Dog purchases his pigeon food from a shop called Birdland. This could be an acknowledgement of the influence of the late Charlie Parker, nicknamed Bird, and to Birdland, the famous jazz club named after Parker. Forest Whitaker, who plays Ghost Dog, played the title role in Clint Eastwood's 1988 film *Bird*. For additional cultural information, see http://en.wikipedia.org/Ghost_Dog.

29 Colin Thompson and Ben Redlich, *The Great Montefiasco* (Melbourne, 2004).

30 Tyson's love of pigeons makes the newspapers. In 2005 he finally won the right to build a pigeon coop in the backyard of his Arizona home following delays over a permit. In some newspapers, this made the front page.

31 Steven J. Simmons and Kim Howard, *Percy to the Rescue* (Watertown, MA, 1998).

32 At www.speedace.info/queen_elizabeth_8_birthday_facts.htm.

The pigeon's name became 'Sandringham Lightning'. The Queen is the patron of a number of racing societies, including the Royal Pigeon Racing Association.

33 Miriam Rothschild, *Butterfly Cooing Like A Dove* (London, 1991), p. 122.
34 Ibid., p. 187.
35 Jan Morris, *A Venetian Bestiary* (London, 1982), pp. 28, 31.
36 I am grateful to Clive D. L. Wynne, *Do Animals Think?* (Princeton and Oxford, 2004), p. 147, for this insight.

5 EXPLOITATION OR CONSERVATION: OUR 'FEATHERED CONSCIENCE'

Wildlife author John Ruthven referred to Martha, the last passenger pigeon, as this 'feathered conscience', cited in Christopher Cokinos, *Hope is the Thing with Feathers* (New York, 2000), p. 274.

1 Lewis Carroll, *Alice's Adventures in Wonderland* (Middlesex, 1965), p. 37.
2 David Day, *The Doomsday Book of Animals* (London, 1981), p. 27.
3 Richard Ellis, *No Turning Back: The Life and Death of Animal Species* (New York, 2004), p. 162.
4 J. C. Greenway, *Extinct and Vanishing Birds of the World* (1958), cited in Ellis, *No Turning Back*, p. 162. Greenway continues, saying that the Portuguese term *duodo*, 'simpleton', was probably not applied to the bird and that there are no references to the dodo bird in Portuguese. The Dutch sometimes called them *walck-vogel*, 'disgusting bird', which may refer to their flavour.
5 Ibid., p. 163.
6 Errol Fuller, *Dodo: From Extinction to Icon* (London, 2002), cited in Ellis, *No Turning Back*, p. 163.
7 Day, *The Doomsday Book of Animals*, pp. 29–30.
8 Ibid., p. 30.
9 Ibid.
10 Ibid.
11 Ibid., p. 31.
12 Ibid.

13 Ibid., p. 273.

14 Gerald Durrell, *Golden Bats and Pink Pigeons* (London, 1977), p. 16.

15 Cokinos, *Hope is the Thing with Feathers*, p. 198.

16 Ellis, *No Turning Back*, p. 173.

17 Virginia C. Holmgren, *Bird Walk through the Bible* (New York, 1972), p. 92.

18 Cokinos, *Hope is the Thing with Feathers*.

19 Ibid., p. 200.

20 Ibid.

21 Ibid., p. 203.

22 Ibid., p. 204.

23 Ibid., p. 207.

24 Ibid., pp. 207–8.

25 Ibid., p. 208.

26 Ibid.

27 Ibid.

28 Fruit of forest trees, such as oaks, chestnuts and beech. Mast is collected and used as a food source for pigs.

29 A pouch-like structure, created by a widening of the oesophagus in birds, where the process of digestion begins. Food is stored in the crop, softened and partially digested before passing into the glandular stomach and then into the gizzard.

30 Cokinos, *Hope is the Thing with Feathers*, p. 201.

31 Ibid.

32 Ibid., p. 209.

33 *Niles Republican*, 29 April 1843.

34 Cokinos, *Hope is the Thing with Feathers*, p. 211.

35 Ibid., p. 217.

36 Ibid., p. 213.

37 Scott Russell Sanders, ed., *Audubon Reader* (Bloomington, IN, 1986), pp. 120–21. Although the year and date of this visit is unclear, in Audubon's writings about the passenger pigeon he mentions visiting other trapping sites in the autumn of 1813, so this record could be from 1813. If not, it is certainly from the times when the passenger pigeon was plentiful. Audubon's writings thrilled readers

and hearers of his papers. He read his paper on the passenger pigeon of America before the Royal Society of Edinburgh on 19 February 1824. Later, Charles Waterton, an eccentric English naturalist who envied his work, tried to discredit Audubon, suggesting that his writing on the passenger pigeon was pure fiction. Duff Hart-Davis, *Audubon's Elephant* (London, 2004), p. 89.
38 Cokinos, *Hope is the Thing with Feathers*, p. 213.
39 Ibid., p. 215.
40 Ellis, *No Turning Back*, p. 173.
41 Cokinos, *Hope is the Thing with Feathers*, p. 215.
42 Officially banned; unofficially trapshooting still goes on in various regions of the United States.
43 Cokinos, *Hope is the Thing with Feathers*, p. 222.
44 Ibid., pp. 228–57.
45 Ibid., p. 244.
46 Ibid., p. 257.
47 Ibid., p. 260.
48 Ibid., p. 263.
49 Ibid., p. 264.
50 Ibid., p. 267.
51 Ibid., p. 271.
52 Ibid., p. 270.
53 Day, *The Doomsday Book of Animals*, p. 38.
54 Ibid.
55 Ibid.
56 Ibid., p. 40. Day also mentions the blue dove found on St Helena, which was extinct by 1775. Little is known about this bird – so little that a name has not been given to it.
57 Ibid.
58 Ibid.
59 Durrell, *Golden Bats and Pink Pigeons*, p. 19.
60 Ibid., p. 40.
61 Ibid.
62 Ibid., p. 45.

Bibliography

Adcock, Fleur, and Jacqueline Simms, eds, *The Oxford Book of Creatures* (Oxford, 1997)

Abs, Michael, ed., *Physiology and Behaviour of the Pigeon* (London, 1983)

Adams, Michelle Medlock, *Memories of the Manger* (Nashville, TN, 2005)

Allan, Nicholas, *The Dove* (London, 2004)

Andersen, Hans Christian, *The Complete Illustrated Stories* (London, 1983)

Armstrong, Edward A., *The Life and Lore of the Bird: In Nature, Art, Myth and Literature* (New York, 1975)

Attenborough, David, *The Life of Birds* (London, 1998)

Ayres, Pam, *Bertha and the Racing Pigeon* (London, 1979)

Baker, Jeannie, *Millicent* (London, 1980)

—, *Home in the Sky* (London, 2003)

Balcombe, Jonathan, *Pleasurable Kingdom: Animals and the Nature of Feeling Good* (Basingstoke, 2006)

Baxter, Ron, *Bestiaries and their Users in the Middle Ages* (Phoenix Mill, MI, 1998)

Bell, David N., *Wholly Animals: A Book of Beastly Tales* (Kalamazoo, MI, 1992)

Bell, Krista, and Ann James, *Pidge* (St Leonards, 1997)

Bell, Krista, and David Miller, *Lofty's Mission* (Sydney, 2008)

Bennett, Arnold, *The Old Wives' Tale* (London, 1935)

Blechman, Andrew D., *Pigeons* (New York, 2006)

Blough, D. S., 'Pigeon Perception of Letters of the Alphabet', *Science*, 218 (1982), pp. 397–8

Bodenheimer, F. S., *Animal and Man in Bible Lands* (Leiden, 1960)

—, *Animal and Man in Bible Lands*: *Figures and Plates* (Leiden, 1972)

Borowski, Oded, *Every Living Thing: Daily Use of Animals in Ancient Israel* (London, 1998)

Brown, Danny, *A Guide to Pigeon, Doves and Quail* (South Tweed Heads, NSW, 1995)

Campbell, Joseph, *The Masks of God: Primitive Mythology*, 4 vols (New York, 1959–68)

Cansdale, George, *Animals of Bible Lands* (Exeter, 1970)

Carroll, Lewis, *The Works of Lewis Carroll* (Middlesex, 1968)

Chiasson, Robert B., *Laboratory Anatomy of the Pigeon*, 3rd edn (Dubuque, IA, 1984)

Cleasby, Kevin, ed. and revd, *Pigeon Classics*, vol. I, *Eaton's Treatise on Pigeons* (Perth, 1997)

—, *Pigeon Classics*, vol. II, *Pigeons: Selby, Tegetmeier and Darwin* (Perth, 1997)

—, *Pigeon Classics*, vol. III, *Fulton and Lumley's Illustrated Book of Pigeons* (Perth, 2001)

—, *Pigeon Classics*, vol. IV, *Fulton and Lumley's Illustrated Book of Pigeons* (Perth, 2007)

—, *Pigeon Genetics for Beginners* (Victoria Park, 1999)

Collodi, Carlo, *Pinocchio* (New York, 2005)

Cokinos, Christopher, *Hope is the Thing with Feathers* (New York, 2000)

Cooper, J. C., ed., *Brewer's Book of Myth and Legend* (London, 1992)

Couzens, Dominic, *Birds by Behaviour* (London, 2003)

Crome, Francis, and James Shields, *Parrots and Pigeons of Australia* (Sydney, 1992)

Curley, Michael J., trans., *Physiologus* (Austin, TX, and London, 1979)

Darwin, Charles, *The Illustrated Origin of Species*, abridged and introduced by Richard E. Leakey (London, 1979)

Day, David, *The Doomsday Book of Animals* (London, 1981)

D'Lacey, Chris, *Fly, Cherokee, Fly* (London, 1998)

Durrell, Gerald, *Golden Bats and Pink Pigeons* (London, 1977)

Eaton, John, *The Circle of Creation: Animals in the Light of the Bible* (London, 1995)

Ellis, Richard, *No Turning Back: The Life and Death of Animal Species* (New York, 2004)

Farmer, David Hugh, *The Oxford Dictionary of Saints*, 2nd edn (Oxford, 1987)

Ferguson, Walter W., *Living Animals of the Bible* (New York, n.d.)

Firth, H. J., *Pigeons and Doves of Australia* (Rigby, 1982)

Foster, Benjamin R., ed. and trans., *The Epic of Gilgamesh* (New Haven, CT, 2001)

Freeman, Don, *Fly High, Fly Low* (New York, 1957)

Gardiner, Juliet, *The Animals' War* (London, 2006)

George, Isabel, and Rob Lloyd Jones, *Animals at War* (London, 2006)

Gibbs, Laura, trans., *Aesop's Fables* (Oxford, 2002)

Gotfryd, Bernard, *Anton the Dove Fancier* (London, 1980)

Graham, Bob, *How to Heal a Broken Wing* (London, 2008)

Green-Armytage, Stephen, *Extraordinary Pigeons* (New York, 2004)

Grindley, Sally, *Feather Wars* (London, 2003)

Habegger, Larry, and Amy G. Carlson, *The Gift of Birds* (San Francisco, CA, 1999)

Hansell, Peter and Jean Hansell, *Doves and Dovecotes* (Bath, 1988)

Hansen, Ian, and John Winch, *Leonardo: Pigeon of Siena* (Sydney, 1998)

Hart-Davis, Duff, *Audubon's Elephant* (London, 2004)

Harter, Walter, *Birds in Fact and Legend* (New York, 1979)

—, *Feathered Heroes: Pigeons from Ancient Times to Now* (New York, 1968)

Hill, Anthony, *Animal Heroes* (Camberwell, 2005)

Holmgren, Virginia C., *Bird Walk through the Bible* (New York, 1972)

Jenson, Philip P., 'The Levitical Sacrificial System', in *Sacrifice in the Bible*, ed. Roger T. Beckwith and Martin J. Selman (Grand Rapids, MI, 1995), pp. 25–31

Kilgower, Ian, and Robert Kilgower, *Australian Racing Pigeons* (Adelaide, 1982)

Kinmonth, Patrick, and Reg Cartwright, *Mr Potter's Pigeon* (London, 1996)

Kligerman, Jack, *A Fancy for Pigeons* (New York, 1978)

König, Karl, *Swans and Storks, Sparrows and Doves* (Edinburgh, 1987)

Kovner, Abba, *My Little Sister* (London, 1971)

Levi, Wendell Mitchell, *The Pigeon* (Columbia, SC, 1941)

—, *Making Pigeons Pay* (New York, 1946)

Lochhead, Marion, *The Battle of the Birds and other Celtic Tales* (Edinburgh, 1981)

Marshall, Rob, *Health Programmes for Racing and Show Pigeons* (Carlingford, 1997)

Martin, David, *Mister P. and his Remarkable Flight* (Lane Cove, NSW, 1975)

Mercatante, Anthony S., *Encyclopedia of World Mythology and Legend* (Frenchs Forest, NSW, 1988)

Milgrom, Jacob, *Leviticus 1–16: A New Translation with Introduction and Commentary* (New York, 1991)

Morris, Jan, *A Venetian Bestiary* (London, 1982)

Mukerji, Dhan Gopal, *Gay-Neck: The Story of a Pigeon* (London, 1938)

Naether, Carl A., *The Book of the Pigeon and of the Wild Foreign Doves*, 5th edn (New York, 1964)

—, *Pigeons* (Neptune City, NJ, 1984)

Nozedar, Adele, *The Secret Language of Birds: A Treasury of Myths, Folklore and Inspirational True Stories* (London, 2006)

Osman, Colin, *Racing Pigeons* [1957] (London, 1980)

Pinney, Roy, *The Animals in the Bible* (Philadelphia, PA, 1964)

Porter, D., and A. Neuringer, 'Musical Discrimination by Pigeons', *Journal of Experimental Psychology: Animal Behavior Processes*, X (1984), pp. 138–48

Potter, Beatrix, *The Tale of the Faithful Dove* (London and New York, 1971)

Rammell, S. Kelly, and Jeanette Conyon, *City Beats: A Hip-Hoppy Pigeon Poem* (Nevada City, CA, 2006)

Ransome, Arthur, *Pigeon Post* [1936] (Harmondsworth, 1969)

Roberts, M. F., *Pigeons* (New York, 1956)

Roberts, M.D.L, and V. E. Gale, *Pigeons, Doves and Dovecotes*
(Kennerleigh, Devon, 2000)

Room, Adrian, ed. and revd, *Brewer's Dictionary of Phrase and Fable*
(London, 2001)

Rothschild, Miriam, *Butterfly Cooing like a Dove* (London, 1991)

Sanders, Scott Russell, ed., *Audubon Reader: The Best Writings of John
James Audubon* (Bloomington, IN, 1986)

Saunders, Nicholas J., *Animal Spirits* (London, 1995)

Sax, Boria, *The Parliament of Animals: Anecdotes and Legends from
Books of Natural History, 1775–1900* (New York, 1992)

Simmons, Steven J., and Kim Howard, *Percy to the Rescue*
(Watertown, MA, 1998)

Singer, Isaac Bashevis, 'Pigeons', in *A Friend of Kafka and Other Stories*
(London, 1972)

Thompson, Colin, and Ben Redlich, *The Great Montefiasco*
(Melbourne, 2004)

Vincent, Mike, *Queensland Homing Society 1894–1994: A Century of
Flying* (Brisbane, 1994)

Vriends, Matthew M., and Tommy E. Erskine, *Pigeons* (New York,
2005)

Watanabe, S., J. Sakamoto and M. Wakita, 'Pigeons' Discrimination
of Paintings by Monet and Picasso', *Journal of the Experimental
Analysis of Behavior*, LXII/2 (1995), pp. 165–74Westwood, Jennifer,
and Jacqueline Simpson, *The Lore of the Land: A Guide to England's
Legends, from Spring-Heeled Jack to the Witches of Warboys* (London,
2005)

Wharton, William, *Birdy* (Harmondsworth, 1979)

White, E. B., *The Points of My Compass* (London, 1963)

White, Gilbert, *The Illustrated Natural History of Selborne* [1789]
(London, 1981)

White, T. H., *The Sword in the Stone* [1938] (London, 1976)

Willems, Mo, *The Pigeon Wants a Puppy!* (London, 2008)

Wright Campbell, Robert, *Where Pigeons Go To Die* (Sarasota, FL,
1978)

Wynne, Clive D. L., *Do Animals Think?* (Princeton and Oxford, 2004)

Associations and Websites

There are numerous websites devoted to pigeon racing, keeping and showing fancy pigeons, writing of their role during the World Wars, and selling books and collectibles. There are also sites that concentrate on one aspect, such as passenger pigeons, or dovecotes.

www.peopleforpigeons.blogspot.com
(follow the envirolink which aims to educate the public and, as a result, improve attitudes towards pigeons)

www.pigeonnetwork.com

www.pigeonpeddler.com

www.pigeons.com.au

www.urbanbirds.org/pigeons

Acknowledgements

I thank the Australian Academy of the Humanities for awarding a grant to assist the publication of *Pigeon*. To my husband, David and son, Rhys, thank you for putting up with squabs and pigeons from the hospital that needed 'a home', while being told they would 'aid my research' for this book; I also appreciate your patience and understanding when I was 'preoccupied.' I thank Professor Katharine Massam, and Dr Linda Marston for their early reading and comments on the first draft of this book. To Dr Sasha Herbert and colleagues at the Lort Smith Animal Hospital for their veterinary advice and support during the writing of this book. To Dave Sudbury, for allowing the use of the lyrics to 'The King of Rome'. To *The World of Wings* Pigeon Center, Oklahoma City, for the use of their library. To Bronwen and Ron, for their enthusiasm and encouragement during the writing of this project. Thank you James Cassar, for showing me your racing pigeons. To my friends, thank you for your patience and interest. This book could not have been written without the ability to draw on previous research undertaken by writers and scholars, poets, artists, filmmakers, past and present. Sixty years on, Wendell Levi's *The Pigeon* is still an outstanding work in this field. To each and every one of you: my heart felt thanks. To Michael Leaman and the dedicated staff at Reaktion Press, you have been fantastic; this closing quote is for you:

'Publishers lead lives as varied and shameless as pigeons, but are less beautiful against the sky.' — E.B. White

Photo Acknowledgements

The author and publishers wish to express their thanks to the below sources for illustrative material and/or permission to reproduce it. (Some information not placed in the captions for reasons of brevity is also given below.)

From Eleazar Albin, *A Supplement to the Natural History of Birds*, vol. II (London, 1740): p. 42; courtesy of the author: pp. 35, 36, 45, 73, 118, 125, 135, 173, 178, 182, 184; photo Lt Bainbridge/Imperial War Museum, London: p. 114; from Pierre Boitard et Corbie, *Les Pigeons de voliere et de colombier, ou histoire naturelle et monographie des pigeons domestiques, renfermant la nomenclature et la description de toutes les races et variétés constantes connues jusquà ce jour; la manière d'etablir des colmbiers et volièrs; d'élever, soigner les pigeons...* (Paris, 1824): pp. 43, 54; photo Mike Brennan/Scope Features: p. 154; British Museum, London (photos © The Trustees of the British Museum): pp. 21, 62, 81, 84, 92, 141; Musée Carnavalet, Paris (photo © Musee Carnavalet/Roger-Viollet): p. 109; from Mark Catesby, *The Natural History of Carolina, Florida and the Bahama Islands...*, vol. I (London 1731): p. 22; photo Mike Charity/Rex Features: p. 51; from William Daniell, *Interesting Selections from Animated Nature*, vol. II (London, 1809): p. 177; from Charles Darwin, *The Variation of Animals and Plants under Domestication*, vol. I (London, 1868): p. 34; from E. S. Dixon, *The Dovecote and the Aviary* (London, 1851): pp. 74, 97; photo ©

Index